T0381298

A LEGACY OF LOVE

The Soundtrack of My Mind

SUSAN BERK WITH TANIA KATAN

AuthorHouse™
1663 Liberty Drive
Bloomington, IN 47403
www.authorhouse.com
Phone: 1 (800) 839-8640

Published by AuthorHouse 08/17/2018

ISBN: 978-1-5462-3827-0 (sc)
ISBN: 978-1-5462-3828-7 (e)
ISBN: 978-1-5462-3829-4 (hc)

Library of Congress Control Number: 2018904717

Print information available on the last page.

Any people depicted in stock imagery provided by Getty Images are models,
and such images are being used for illustrative purposes only.
Certain stock imagery © Getty Images.

This book is printed on acid-free paper.

CONTENTS

DEDICATION

To my loving husband, Lee Eliot Berk who, with his patience, deep listening, support and understanding, has guided us through years of courtship, friendship and marriage. Because our marriage is made up of music, musicians and life's sweetest melodies, I'd like to dedicate these 3 songs to Lee:

1. "Thank You for The Music" lyrics by Benny Anderson and Björn Ulvaeus of ABBA
2. Two for the Road" by Henry Mancini (Henry and his wife Ginny's favorite song)
3. "Our Love Is Here to Stay" by George Gershwin

There's a little Gershwin story that relates to Lee's life. Lee's father, Lawrence Berk, who founded Berklee College of Music, was a student of Joseph Schillinger's (1895 – 1943) in New York City as was George Gershwin. Also, our family has a portrait of George Gershwin by Andy Warhol, which was part of Warhol's series, *Portraits of Jews of the Twentieth Century.*

This is for you, Lee, for a wonderful life that has literally brought music to my ears.

INTRODUCTION

"For many, pop songs that are deeply embedded in our consciousness become part of the soundtrack of our lives. An unforgettable melody or a lyric that expresses exactly what we've felt has the power to flood our mind with impressions of joyful moments long past, or to help us get through a rough patch in our lives. People all across the world feel the power of songs that make us want to dance, sing, or lean on them during hard times.
—Mark Small, Editor in Chief of Berklee Today

"Influences at home, including classical music, were not all specifically jazz, but the family radio was always on..."
—Anat Cohen

Music has the power to do many things. For me, music has been there when I needed to escape, to be present, to be loved, and to understand my purpose in life. Music saved my life—many times—and made it more meaningful. Music helped me to find the love of my life, gave me hope, and led me to you, my grandchildren.

I'd like to share this legacy of music with you while I'm still here, while we're still sharing this earth together, in hopes that when I'm no longer here in body, the aura of music and musical memories I leave to you resonates beyond this lifetime. Music is your inheritance.

Even the process of creating this book is like a real-time Jazz improvisation! I meet with Tania (or send her recordings) and share stories about meeting your grandfather for the first time, meeting your parents for the first time, and meeting you for the first time. I share songs like, "If You Knew Susie" and others that made me question my name and find my voice. We try to find the threads that weave in and out of the life I've created with your grandfather, your parents, you, and with music. My inheritance has been one of frizzy hair, bipolar disorder, deep love of music and you. There have been times in my life when I've been faced with the stigma of mental illness, times when I fought to stay afloat, putting on a brave face until my mind caught up with the plan. There have been times when I felt like the queen of jazz, meeting some of my favorite musicians in the world. Whether you're feeling like the queen or king of something, or donning a mask until you feel comfortable enough to take it off, I want you to know that being different is what it means to be human. Being different is what makes a great jazz musician, great.

I have always been great at orchestrating events. All the pieces of an event, all the pieces in an orchestra are equally important; you have to know what they'll sound like individually and together in order to create harmony. That's why this book feels important to me; it's my half of a conversation with you. Half of a dialogue. Me talking, you listening, and then we'll switch. The talking and the listening are equally important. The listening allows us to be moved by the music and the music moves us through the stories that make up our lives.

I've set out to write a memoir that is like an album because music has created the foundation for my entire life. More specifically, jazz music. But you know this. You know that the home Papa and I have created is really the house that jazz built. You know this because you are our children and grandchildren. You know this because you grew up listening to Arturo, Chick and Herb. You know this because from the time you could walk you wandered the hallways of a school filled with music, a school named after Lee, Berklee.

This book uses grammar expansively. It's less of a literary piece and more of a colloquial expression. So, if you see inconsistencies in punctuation, capitalization, proper names, or any other disruption in the structure of language…good! Sometimes it's good to disrupt structures in order to create a space for everyone to speak their minds or to sing their truths.

This book is a gift to you, my children and grandchildren, so that you might learn a little more about Lee and me and maybe, in turn, learn a little more about you. This book is a gift to myself, too. Usually people give gifts like earrings or watches or flowers, but you'll find that most of the gifts that Papa and I give are of a different nature. We give gifts that nurture people and places. We give gifts of art, education, music and stories.

Now, before we go any further I want to introduce you to Tania Katan, who has been working with me to extract and develop the stories in this book. Tania… take it away!

Hello, Rachel, Julia, Louisa and Ethan! Nice to meet all of you. And, if you don't mind, I'll be talking in italics under the heading "Musical Notes" so you know that it's me and not your Noni, ok? Great. It is such a treat to meet with your Noni once a month as well as listening to the stories she has recorded on her phone. We meet in the library at Sagewood. Sagewood is the name of the life care services senior complex where your grandparents live. The library has tall ceilings and in the center of the space is a strong, dark wood table. The table is surrounded by bookshelves with books that have been donated by the residents of Sagewood. Your Noni always gives me a hug when I first see her and when we part. She always asks, "Do you need water? I brought you water." Then she asks, "So… how are you doing?" She asks this with a big smile. Her eyes light up. Your Noni is so clearly driven by learning. In addition to leaving a legacy of stories and wisdom for you, she and your grandfather are leaving a legacy of education, of art, of curiosity and music for generations of people who wouldn't otherwise have the opportunity to learn, to pursue, to BE.

Together your grandparents have created a life of learning and giving. They've set up scholarships for need-based students pursuing music, served on boards that shifted the way women are represented in the arts, helped veterans suffering from shell shock develop coping skills, started Friends of Santa Fe Jazz, and Woody's Place at Sagewood. They have brought attention to depression and bipolar disorder in ways that enliven people enduring these diagnoses. Your grandparents are grand, indeed! Which is to say that they are important and magnificent human beings.

During one of our meetings, Susan tells me she always wanted to be an archaeologist and dig. I tell her she's constantly excavating, extracting information by asking perceptive questions. One of her major regrets in life is that her parents and grandparents didn't take the time to share their stories, leaving her with many gaps and questions. Her father was a musician whom she never heard play. Her mother was the president of a library yet rarely read to her. Her grandfather was missing half of his finger and no one ever asked why. Can you imagine that? What if your grandfather, Lee, showed up to your house and was missing half a finger and didn't say why?! Wouldn't you want to know? Because your Noni's life as a youngster was filled with half-stories, she wants to give you the whole story.

Your Noni loves sharing stories with people; she's a connecter. The act of her sharing the story is just as important as the story itself. So, my job is to receive her stories, to be the recipient of your grandmother's narratives. She has many stories. Once, your grandmother saved a young woman from suicide by getting her into a treatment facility. Once, your grandmother wanted to be social director on a cruise ship. Once, your grandmother said, "I love teamwork… as long as I'm in charge." Once, your grandmother told me, "You have to start somewhere!" So, let's start with music. And just so you know, we are going to bounce around in this book, because music and memories can be bouncy. Is that ok with you? Good!

September In The Rain

Close your eyes and picture a vinyl record. See the deep grooves running in circles. See the light hit its shiny black surface and reflect back out onto the world. There is an entire world on that record. There is an entire family on that record. A family of songs strung together by a theme. These songs have been assembled by producers and musicians. These songs have been recorded, mixed and mastered for you to listen to, for you to enjoy, for you to lose yourself in. Each song has been etched into this album. Each song represents a moment in time, a memory, a story, a world.

Keep your eyes closed and imagine sitting in your living room next to a record player, surrounded by your family. Your hand is on the arm of the record player about to drop the needle. As soon as the needle hits the top edge of the record, you'll be releasing the songs, the memories, one at a time, into the world. Can you feel the tension between the spinning record and that exacting needle? Go ahead and gently drop the arm. As the needle hits a deep groove, notice how it gives way to the scratch, pop, crackle, snap of a song. What song do you hear? Is it "To Wait For Love" by Herb Alpert & The Tijuana Brass? Is it "What a Wonderful World" by Louis Armstrong? Is it "Eternal Child" by Chick Corea's Elektric Band?

As your head moves in time to the music, do you notice any moments when the needle gets stuck on a song? When the song begins to skip? *And I think to myself. And I think to myself. And I think to myself. And I think to myself.* Quickly pick up the arm of the record player and place it on another part of the song …*what a wonderful world.* What does it feel like when the song is skipping? How do you feel once the song is back on track?

Open your eyes. Pick up the album cover that is face up on the floor looking at you and look inside of it. Did you find liner notes? Liner notes is a piece of paper filled with short stories that celebrate the making of a song, some fun facts about the band, and maybe an essay.

If your life were an album, what would it look like? What would be the theme? What songs would you choose to be on the record? How would you order them? Would you start with a song you could tap your toes to? When would the needle skip and call attention to moments of discord? What would be the title of your album?

If my life were an album, the theme would be: Love and Music. The title of the album would be "The Soundtrack of My Mind." The first song on the record would be "September In the Rain" because it's a jazz standard that everyone from Sarah Vaughn to Nora Jones to The Beatles has recorded. Plus, I was born in September.

On September 12, 1947 there was definitely music in the air.
- Miles Davis All-Stars debuts at The Savoy Ballroom.
- Louis Armstrong performs at Carnegie Hall.
- Henri Matisse's book *Jazz* is published.
- I am born. A lover of jazz in utero. Let's just say…I was hip to the jive before I was even alive!

On September 12, 1947 my mother's hero, Dr. Edward Comstock, brought me into this world by way of Lawrence Memorial Hospital in New London, Connecticut. He used forceps to grab my little head and pull me out of the birth canal. The forceps left my face distorted for a long time and led me to question whether or not I would ever be beautiful. I never knew how much I weighed. My mom was so enamored with Dr. Edward that she named my brother Marc Edward when he was born in 1953.

In contrast, both of our daughters, Nancy and Lucy, were natural births. I had taken Lamaze classes with Lee and both times I was ready to give birth to my babies. Nancy Jeanette Berk was born on August 15, 1976, 7 lbs. 6 ounces and Lucy Georgia Berk was October 7, 1979, 7 lbs. 9 ounces. Both were beautiful!

I am a Virgo, which means that I am loyal, analytical, kind, hardworking, and practical. I love healthy food, books, nature, and cleanliness. I dislike rudeness, asking for help and taking center stage. I pay attention to the smallest details and create spaces for everyone to shine. I was born Susan Miller Ginsberg. I am now Susan Berk. I'm a wife, mother, grandmother, Virgo, and lover of music. What more do you need to know?

<ins>If You Knew Susie</ins>

"How simple a thing it seems to me that to know ourselves as we are, we must know our mothers' names."
-Alice Walker

As you know, my name is Susan, but did you know that my father used to call me Susie? There was a song written long before you were born called, "If You Knew Susie" and it went like this: *If you knew Susie, like I know Susie Oh! Oh! Oh! What a girl!* I loved that song; it made me feel so good, so alive! They called me Susie as a little girl and even in college my roommates, Nancy Jo and Patty, used to call me Susie. There was a moment in high school when people called me Sue, because of the song by Dion, "Runaround Sue."

At the time I thought that Dion's Sue and I were similar, always busy, running around, in motion, like the song, "Poetry In Motion", *walkin' by my side, her lovely locomotion, keeps my eyes open wide.* But then I grew up and realized that the Sue who was running around in the song was up to no good, so I started to detest being called Sue and wanted to be called Susan. S is also for Susan, and there are lots of songs with Susan and Susanna in them.

Oh, Susanna
Now, don't you cry for me
As I come from Alabama with this banjo on my knee

My father would sing a song to me that had another S-word in it, sweet.
Oh ain't she sweet,
Well see her walking down that street.
Well I ask you very confidentially,
Ain't she sweet?

Whenever my father sang that song to me, it made me feel special. It's the same feeling I get when we're on the phone and I ask you, Rachel, Julia, Louisa and Ethan to sing to me. Sometimes we sing for 30 minutes and it's out of tune and pure joy! I ask, "Will you sing me a song?" And Louisa will sing, "Twinkle, twinkle, little star…" And then we'll sing…
Zip-A-Dee-Doo-Dah
Zip-A-Dee-A
My oh my, what a wonderful day!

And more singing…
Six little ducks that I once knew
Fat ones, skinny ones, fair ones too.
But the one little duck with the feather on his back
He led the others with his quack, quack, quack.

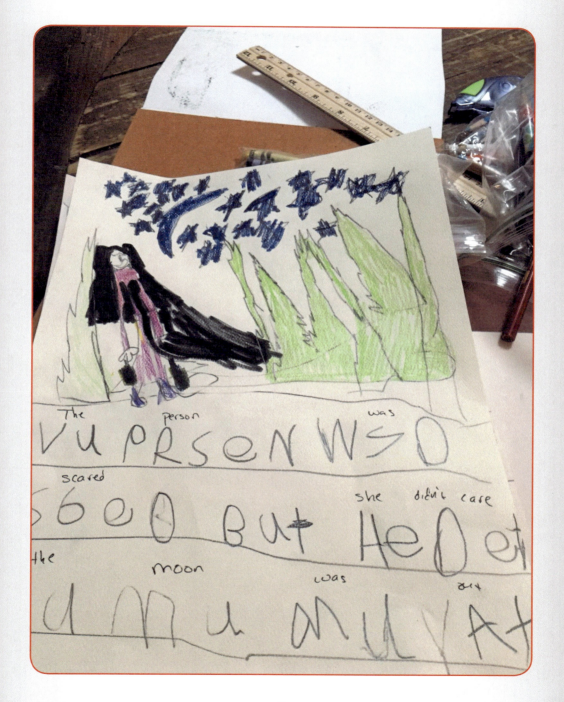

The person was
VUPRSeNWSO
scared
SbeO But HeOet she didn't care
the moon was air
uMuMiLVA+

9

Noni's Jazz Improvisation

Throughout this book you will find Noni's Jazz Improvisations, which are invitations for you kids to engage in fun, creative exercises. Remember, this book is an album, which means that we take turns singing and dancing, talking and listening. So, these improvisations are your turn to sing and mine to listen. And, like any great jazz improvisation, there are some simple rules:

1. Make mistakes often and celebrate them!
2. Try your best.
3. Listen carefully so you know how to add your special flair into the mix!

I have a question for you: Do you know of any songs with your name in them? Like, for example, "I Love Louisa" by Fred Astaire or The Beatles' song, "Julia" or "Rachel's Song" by James McMurtry or "Happy Birthday, Ethan" by your family.   Play that song! How does it make you feel when you hear it? When you sing it? Are there songs that have yet to be written about you? I want you to try on a song, like you would try on a t-shirt or pants or shoes. Take a few minutes to find a song with your name in it. Listen to it and see how it makes you feel, how it fits on you. If you can't find a song that feels like a good fit; write your own song! Ready…GO!

Soundtrack of My Mind

Songs are like a trail of biographical breadcrumbs that family leaves for us to discover. Music can help us find our way when we go astray. It can lead us to find new adventures and meaning in life.

It's a ritual. A ceremony. From Buddhist chanting to Jazz. Music speaks to us. Jazz musicians are communicating through drums and saxophone, bass and vocals, notes and the space in between notes.

Music has been a part of our family. My grandparents, the Millers, had an RCA Victrola with 33 ½ RPM records, those little black discs made of vinyl and carrying the weight of opera, classical, and jazz. We danced for hours listening to those fine albums. My grandfather George would proudly say that he owned stock in RCA.

The Ginsbergs, meanwhile, had a very old Victrola with a horn and scratchy needle. I think the needle on George's set was a diamond needle. The Ginsbergs played mostly Jewish music, however my dad, David, loved music so much he joined a band playing the saxophone and clarinet in New York City with Henry

Pasnik who later changed his name to Henry Jerome of the Henry Jerome Orchestra. The orchestra in which Alan Greenspan the famous economist and former chairman of the Federal Reserve Bank played saxophone. Henry was from Norwich, Connecticut and he was introduced to Dad through Dad's cousin, Norman Israelite, who was a student at Norwich Free Academy or NFA. Dad travelled to New York City to play. He spoke highly of his years playing society dance music. However, I never heard my father play his instruments. Once he became a doctor of optometry I think he must have let the past disappear. His instrument was a distant memory by the time I fell in love with music.

Both Mom and Dad loved music; they would leave the stereo on all day even if the house were empty of family members. Lyrics and tunes (and occasional dancing) became replacements for conversations that needed to happen. Our family rarely used language to express emotions. My parents never said, "I love you." But I do remember my dad singing to me, songs like, "If you knew Susie" and "Ain't She Sweet." Even though my voice is off key, I still love singing because it brings so much joy! When I was a kid in elementary school my music teacher told me to, "Mime the singing. Just pretend."

It doesn't matter if I'm miming, singing off key or listening to music, it all plays a part in composing the soundtrack of my mind.

Noni's Jazz Improvisation

Everyone feels embarrassed about something and wishes they didn't have it or it didn't happen to them. Part of me wishes I didn't have bipolar disorder. But I've worked with it and made it a positive. And people with bipolar and mental illness can be very creative people. That's me. They can be very sweet people. That's me. They can be very kind and think of others. So I want you to make a list of all the things that make you feel embarrassed or that you wish you didn't have. And now I want you to pick one of those things and make another list of all the really great things that you have as a result of having that thing. So, if your thing is: *Really Big Ears*, maybe the great things are:

1. I can hear better
2. I like touching the pointy part on top when I'm nervous
3. I kind of look like that really great elf character I love in that book.

You get the point. Go for it!

Jelly Roll and Ice Cream, Please

"My advice to you is not to inquire why or whither, but just enjoy your ice cream while it's on your plate. That's my philosophy."

-Thornton Wilder

Jazz has a history of merging food with music. Charles Mingus sang "Jelly Roll," Chet Baker's "Tasty Pudding," Tony Scott and Bill Evans' "Vanilla Frosting on Beef Pie," and so many more. In fact, your Noni has merged food and jazz for years, feeding some of the most highly-regarded jazz musicians of our time, nourishing them before and after their performances, like George Benson, Jeff Hamilton, Arturo Sandoval and so many more. You might be curious as to what my favorite food is. Well, my favorite food is—after vegetables and fruits, of course—ice cream!

Here's a brief history of my big, enormous, gigantic LOVE of ice cream. It began when I was a little girl, probably Louisa's age. I would visit my maternal grandparents, George and Gloria Miller in Bristol,

Connecticut and every Sunday my Poppop and I would walk down the hill to the local sundry shop while my grandmother, Goldie, stayed behind preparing a treat for our return: coffee milk. Sipping that sweet, light brown milk made me feel so grown up. Poppop would give me one nickle to pay for and pick out any ice cream I wanted. Can you imagine buying your favorite ice cream with five cents? Can you imagine buying ANYTHING with five cents? This was at a time when a five-cent piece could buy you an entire world. If you had a nickel you could buy chewing gum, a postcard, five pieces of candy, a stamp, and ice cream! I took Poppop's five cents and purchased the most beautiful chocolate-coated vanilla ice cream on a stick that was ever made. That glorious frozen treat became my favorite ice cream of all time! That was until I grew up a little bit and discovered the Good Humor man.

In my hometown, New London, Connecticut, the Good Humor man would cruise by in his truck ringing a bell, yelling, "Ice cream, ICE CREAM!" Or he'd ride up and down our block on his bicycle, which was rigged with a full freezer in the front, right underneath the handlebars. He would stop and list off the flavors to all the kids who had gathered around him, each excited for their turn to order a sweet, frozen treat. "We've got Jimmy Cones, Cherry Bombs, Creamsicles!" I always knew exactly what I wanted. "I'll have a toasted almond, please!" I LOVED the toasted almond on a stick. It was vanilla ice cream covered in toasted almonds and stuck on a stick. I couldn't imagine anything better than that, not until your great-grandmother, Gussy Ginsberg, made an ice cream dessert that was so outrageously delicious I thought I'd never, ever, EVER eat anything but THAT, ever again! Are you kids ready for this one? Are you sitting down? It is SO big and unbelievably yummy that you just might put down this book and try to make it yourselves. DON'T do it. I repeat, DO NOT attempt to make it yourselves. Ask your parents. For your birthday. It's THAT AMAZING!

Ok, so…Gussy started this dessert by making two, homemade, super fresh, extra-large waffles on her waffle iron griddle. You heard me right. And then, in between those beautiful, crisp-on-the-outside-warm-and-soft-on-the-inside waffles she would plop three scoops of ice cream: chocolate, vanilla AND strawberry. Behold: the waffle ice cream sandwich. Speaking of holding, my little hands could barely wrap around the entire waffle extravaganza. Don't worry; I was able to eat every last bite with a fork and knife.

Growing up, my parents' best friends were the Bakers. Walter and Irma Baker. When your name is Baker, it's as if you were born to design delicious desserts. Walter and Irma leaned into their name and fulfilled their destiny. They owned the Mohegan Dairy in New London, Connecticut where they made the most spectacularly delicious ice cream. Suffice it to say that our freezer was always filled with fresh ice cream from the Bakers. Also, just a bike ride away from our home on Admiral Drive was Michael's Dairy; a red wooden barn that had many scrumptious and unusual ice cream flavors inside, particularly raspberry in a cone. It was as if my love of ice cream, which was already deeply imprinted in my DNA, was brilliantly triggered by the place in which I grew up. In other words, location became the needle that gently dropped into my ice cream groove!

I remember being in Moscow, Russia in 1968 with a student group. Of course we had to check out the local ice cream parlor and what we discovered was…Russians serve ice cream with champagne. I was in heaven! But don't get any ideas; you're too young for that combo. In Moscow, we also found ice cream with real vanilla bean at the GUM department store. It was just like the kind they served in Philadelphia at the Reading Market.

During my high school years, our mellifluous destination was Friendly's Family Restaurant. Who knew they even served burgers and sandwiches, we only went for the Fribble. They had this very very thick thick milkshake called the Fribble. It was served in a thick clear glass with thick red letters printed on the side that read, *Fribble. The Friendly thick, thick shake.* It was a hybrid between a milkshake and soft serve. If you stuck your straw into the Fribble, it would stand perfectly still for minutes. We had to suck so hard just to get the milk shake to break loose and move through the straw. One time they were so friendly at Friendly's that they served me an extra-large Fribble, it was so large, in fact, that I was forced to share it with a friend.

In 1969, I did something not so good. Ok, it was pretty bad. I was in college and on a quiet Monday evening, after classes, a group of friends and I went to The Chat, a little café next to the school cafeteria, and what we did next is what made me a not-so-good-girl, but it's important that I tell you about it, so here it goes… We stole 2 enormous containers of ice cream from The Chat! I'm pretty sure that each container had 3 gallons of ice cream in it. That's 6 gallons of ice cream. When you kids go to the store and get ice cream, your parents might pick up a pint or a half a gallon or a whole gallon. Now, 1 gallon of ice cream has about 32 servings in it, which means, that if four adorable grandchildren (you) eat ice cream every night (after veggies, of course), you could have ice cream for 8 nights straight. Not too shabby. But if you had 6 gallons of ice cream, all four of you could eat ice cream, every night, for 48 nights! I know what you're thinking, "Noni, that's not so bad, stealing 6 gallons of ice cream." Well, it wasn't the worst thing I've ever done, but I ate so much of the ice cream, much more than one gallon, by myself, that I threw up! Yuck.

Living in Boston, I was well aware that I was in the epicenter of ice cream parlors. Places like Brigham's and Bailey's were everywhere. I remember Bailey's ice cream parlor in Cambridge with its small white swirled marble tables and matching chairs. The backs of the wrought iron chairs were twisted into heart shapes. I loved ordering ice cream sundaes complete with chocolate fudge syrup, whipped cream and a cherry on top. Brighams had a particular specialty as well: jimmies (chocolate sprinkles). I loved jimmies on every flavor of ice cream.

In Japan, I discovered green tea ice cream. In Italy, it was gelato and my favorite flavors as an adult are chocolate chip and mint chip. Other ice cream memories include Howard Johnson's with their 28 flavors, Baskin Robbins with 32 flavors and the famous ice cream cakes at Carvel. But if you ask me, I'll eat any kind of ice cream, anytime of day! Profiteroles, spumoni, toasted almond on a stick, soft serve, frozen yogurt, an ice cream sundae, and even a banana split!

At the end of a day, I love to sit down next to Lee, listen to jazz and dip my spoon into a cold bowl filled with coffee or rum raisin or mint chip ice cream.

Noni's Jazz Improvisation

So, dear grandchildren, are there two things you love so much that you wish you could mush them together, like ice cream and jazz? Is there something sweet you love to eat? Is there an art form you dig enough to dig into? A book you love to read? A movie you love to watch over and over again? A song you long to hear? It's time to invent an ice cream flavor that mashes up the two things you love the most! Will it be: Finding Nemopolitan Ice Cream? How about: Baby Beluga Bubblegum? What new flavor of ice cream and the arts will you invent? I pronounce you: The Inventor of Sweet New Art Treats. Come up with a flavor that has never existed. Time to invent…GO!

Hair

Dizzy Gillespie had a "soul patch" which was a small square of hair under his bottom lip that made him hip. Chick Corea's dark curls were always found cascading down his neck. Bonnie Raitt with her long, red hair and that shock of white running up the middle of it like a stark desert highway. Louis Armstrong sang, "Cause my hair is curly, just because my teeth are pearly…" What does hair mean to you? Sure, it's on your head, sometimes, and sometimes it leaves your head when you least expect it, but do you ever think about it? Do you remember a time before you had hair? When you were really little and only had a few sprigs? Has the color of your hair changed as you've grown up?

My hair has lived several lives. It's been curly, frizzy, dark, short, long, and straight. I've worn it all ways. I've even worn a wig! When your grandfather and I were on a cruise ship and we went snorkeling during the day (which made me and my hair exhausted) I wore a wig at night so when we went out to dinner and then to listen to jazz, my hair looked straight and long and beautiful and wide awake! I loved that wig. Is that weird? To love a wig? It didn't feel weird, it felt right. I loved that wig so much that I had my passport picture and photo for my driver's license taken with the wig on.

Throughout my life my hair has been referred to in many ways, like, *frizzy haired* and *curly topped*. My hair was dark and thick until my late 30's and early 40's, when it decided to turn white without my permission. I used to blow dry my hair. I used Spoolies, rollers, flat irons, anything to make it straight, to keep it down, to help it cling to my neck and fall just below my ears, like Bernice who got a bob in the short story by F. Scott Fitzgerald, "Bernice Bobs Her Hair." Keeping my hair straight was a pain in the butt. I even stopped swimming for fear of messing up my hair. I loved swimming!

I remember the days when, once a week, I would go to the hair salon and Victor would wash my hair, then blow dry it out so it would lie straight. I played this game with myself after going to the salon: *how long could I keep my hair perfectly straight without any kinks or curls.* I never won.

Once I tried henna hair coloring and another time I thought blonds had more fun, so I tried to be blonde (spoiler alert: I didn't have more fun), but most of all I'm happy with my natural color, salt and pepper (heavy on the salt these days). Every once in a while, though, I long to go back and see what I looked like as a brunette.

Hair is important to me. It frames my face, makes me feel good or less good sometimes. Hair makes me feel buoyant or a little less springy, depending on my mood and my hair's mood, too. But nowadays, my hair is short, it's cute, it fits me. Instead of using a brush or comb or curling iron or blow dryer, I simply run my fingers through my hair. It's bouncy just like I am. It bounces when I listen to my favorite songs like, "These Are A Few of My Favorite Things" from The Sound of Music and "What Do You Do With a BA in English" from Avenue Q, "Lovely" from A Funny Thing Happened on the Way to the Forum.

Recently I bought myself a wig as a Christmas/Hanukkah gift. Everyone will know it's a wig because I haven't grown my hair out in years, but I love long hair. Don't worry, the wig matches my natural hair color, I'm not trying to be blonde or brunette or a redhead, I'm just trying to be me, with longer hair.

So, take care of your hair, you've got great genes and great hair. And remember: Your hair is going to change, a lot. Sometimes you will change it; sometimes it will change you. But your hair doesn't run the show, your head does! So, don't let your hair call the shots. Don't give up the things you love, like swimming, skateboarding, cooking, playing because you're having a bad hair day or month or year, stick your foot in the pool and go for a swim anyway!! And anyway, you can always don a hat! Speaking of hats, I love hats: caps, turbans, cotton, velvet, wool, black, brown, beige, gray, blue – you name it – I have it! Thank god for hats; protection from the sun and rain, warmth from the cold, wild and wide brimmed for the cowgirl in me, handmade, straw, beret, funky, matching Vail jazz caps with Papa. I love them all. In fact, one of my favorite children's books to read to Nancy and Lucy was *Caps for Sale*.

Musical Notes: 1

(Noni and Tania are sitting in the Sagewood library discussing the musicality of hair.)

Tania: So, where's the music in hair?

Noni: Well, I'm looking at your hair, Tania, and you've got spiked hair, so that's like rhythm. There's movement in hair, each strand of hair, all going in different directions. When the hair isn't calm or predictable, but goes in different directions, there's movement. I happen to like movement in hair. I like when my hair spikes a little, too. Even the act of preparing your hair to leave the house is musical, the sound of a blow dryer, the rhythm of the brush.

Tania: I hadn't thought about that, it's like a John Cage performance.

Noni: Cutting hair is like a performance. The hairdresser is moving and dancing through your hair. I have a new hairdresser, a woman now, and she's cutting it, not blunt, but cutting into the hair and it's making my hair softer, in fact, when I saw the twins at Thanksgiving I said, 'Feel my hair! Feel my hair! It's not scratchy anymore, it's soft.'

Tania: This is great! The reason why I asked you about the musicality in hair is because we're creating a unifying memoir, so I'm trying to find ways to connect your hair with music.

Susan: I think this memoir is going to have a beginning, but not an ending.

Lead Sheet

"I always try to teach by example and not force my ideas on a young musician. One of the reasons we're here is to be a part of this process of exchange." -Dizzy Gillespie

A lead sheet is a piece of music in its simplest form: melody, chords, and lyrics. It offers musicians a few plot points of interest and then inspires improvisation. A lead sheet encourages musicians to try out different ways of playing the same song. It demands that you let go of everything you know to be true about reading music and follow your heart instead of your head.

I think I've spent my entire life leading by example, not on purpose, just by trying to do good work, allowing a space for improvisation and following my heart. I've always loved organizing, fundraising and developing audiences for good causes. Even today, at 70 years old, I'm still running fundraisers in my community, organizing events, panels and concerts. To me there is no difference between volunteering and being paid for work. When you're doing the work you love, sometimes you get paid for it in money, sometimes you don't. But you always get paid in the joy and feeling of gratitude that it brings. Happiness is its own currency.

My mom and dad were leaders, organizers, planners and charity givers. My grandparents all came from the old country. George Miller from Poland, Louie from Liverpool, Gussy Ginsberg from Germany. Goldie Eisenberg Miller was the only one born in the United States. Both my grandfathers were tailors, which meant they were poor, financially, but rich in spirit, kindness and love of music. They led with their hearts too.

Growing up I worked in my grandfather's store "Millers" a lady's wear shop in Bristol, Connecticut where I sold dresses. I learned how to greet customers, make helpful suggestions, and select the best dresses, sweaters, blouses, and skirts for them. I watched the women's faces light up when they tried on an outfit that made them feel beautiful. How they looked, when they looked in the mirror to see someone they thought was more beautiful than the person who first walked into the shop. This is the look I would recognize later in life on the faces of jazz greats when they let go of the notes and jumped into the flow.

My grandfather, George Miller whom I called Popop, always loved being in the flow of beautiful things, namely architecture and Cadillacs. In fact, he built a two-car garage out of brick, which housed his shiny new Cadillac. It was always shiny and new because every year he traded his old Cadillac in for a new one. He was a fast driver easily annoyed with drivers that placed less emphasis on speed. He raced from West Hartford to Bristol and back every day as if he was competing to win the coveted Borg-Warner Trophy.

In Popop George's shop I learned the art of sales, business techniques and customer service. Popop's office was above the store. A green leather couch created the regal centerpiece of his office. A brown leather chair with wooden arms and legs sat next to the couch. The furniture was as strong and confident as my Popop was. I loved that furniture. Popop had a bookkeeper named Gertrude. He relied on Gertrude as if she was the backbone of his business. And she was. Gertrude was intelligent, good with numbers, and led with grace.

I never remembered my grandmother, Goldie, working in the store. She was the lady of the house, always cooking and volunteering for charity work. Popop George was responsible for building the synagogue in Bristol. His name appeared there, engraved on a silver plaque. Like the deep grooves etched in records, my Popop left his mark in Bristol as a businessman, an upstanding member of the Jewish community and a true mensch.

My skills in customer service, along with my desire to make people feel beautiful and vibrant, bloomed into a love of entrepreneurship. In 1976, when I was in my late 30's I founded a successful destination management business in Boston called, Uncommon Boston. I was the president, had employees and subcontractors and, in the dozen years I ran the company, it was close to becoming a million-dollar business! It wasn't the money that got me excited, though, it was the fact that I had created something from the ground up that engaged and delighted people from all around the world. I produced one-of-a-kind events and experiences that delighted clients and left them wanting more.

Uncommon Boston created customized tours and special events. Everything from "Graveyards and Goodies", to chocolate tours, to paper tours, to art/architecture/music tours. You name it, I've tried it! We gave tours in foreign languages to people of all ages and backgrounds. I worked with corporations, conventions, spouse programs, schools, churches and private individuals. We used limousines, buses, vans, and boats to show people the beauty and vibrancy of Boston. We even hosted parties at historic sites and once held an event at a hair salon! Some of my clients included: IBM, Hewlett Packard, The Four Seasons, Exxon, General Electric, Harvard Business School, MIT, Mitsubishi of Japan, Harrods of London, and more. I was working with the Ritz Carlton, Le Meridian, Marriot Copley, the Fairmont and other luxury hotels to offer visitors uncommon experiences and spaces for their events. Once, we rented Symphony Hall for IBM and brought in Dionne Warwick to perform!

There were so many details in doing this kind of work, relying on caterers, busses, venues, organizations; it was pretty stressful. After an amazing 12-year run, I decided to give it up, but the reputation I had established as someone who is respectful, organized, creative and caring has remained long after Uncommon Boston closed its doors. Because of my business's fine reputation, I was asked to produce a guidebook to Boston and guess what the title of it is? You guessed it: Uncommon Boston. And if you are thinking, "Oh, Noni, that's so cute that you wrote a book." Think again, because we sold 22,000 copies! And if you ask me nicely, I'll share one with you.

I learned so many skills from working in my grandfather's shop and while running Uncommon Boston. These skills are still with me today: accounting, marketing, hiring, firing, sales, and human resources. But really, the most import thing I've learned in my career is that we will all take turns leading and following. As long as we continue to serve others, do good work and allow space to improvise we'll be a *bad* leader (which is *good* in jazz lingo)!

Here are a few jam sessions (aka projects) that I've been proud to improvise with:

- Contributing to the book, *In Our Own Voices: A Guide to Conducting Life History Interview with American Jewish Women*, edited by Jayne K. Guberman and published by the Jewish Women's Archives.
- Volunteering at the Jewish Women's Archives for several years and running a program for the organization in Santa Fe.
- Mentoring the children of homeless women at a church on Newbury Street in Boston.
- Tutoring 1st and 2nd graders in Math and English as part of the Partners in Education program.
- Archivist for the John F. Kennedy Presidential Library. The director of the library, my boss Dan Fenn, was selected by president John F. Kennedy to bring forth the best and brightest for his White House team.
- Assistant Librarian at the American Jewish Historical Society. My bosses, Bernie Wax and Dan Fenn, were also my mentors and are still good friends of mine to this day.
- Volunteering at the National Park Service, which operated JFK's birthplace in Brookline.
- Executive Producer (fundraising and outreach) for the film: *The S Word*, a documentary about suicide (previously I had an association with a documentary "Of Two Minds" about bipolar disorder).
- A board member, then Fundraising Chair, then President of the New Mexico Chapter **of** the National Museum of Women in the Arts, which led me to become a member of National Advisory Board of NMWA.
- Recognized as a community legacy for my work with NMWA. Organized a fashion runway show and sale of women artist jewelry and clothing which raised $25,000. Created "18 Days" a three-weekend long celebration of all the art, poetry, film, theatre, visual art, and music in Santa Fe at the Center For Contemporary Arts. More than 1,000 people came to the opening where we served two types of soup! The crowds stopped traffic on Old Pecos Road and the police had to come. It was a success. In the spirit of jazz improv, Papa and I really get our groove on when we volunteer together! Here are a few places we've focused our time, skills and riffs:
- Papa and I started (and are active in) the philanthropy group: Founding Members of the Producers Circle at the Musical Instrument Museum (MIM) and Friends of MIM at Sagewood.
- Lee started a chess club at Sagewood.
- At Sagewood, I act as a self-appointed cultural ambassador.

- Lee started a jazz appreciation party and award for those in Arizona who support and nurture jazz.
- Both of us have served on the Arizona Leadership Council of Mayo Clinic. We support the Sandra Day O'Conner Institute and the Phoenix Conservatory of Music. I am also a proud and active member of Arizona State University Women and Philanthropy.
- Lee served on the board of the New Mexico School for the Arts and SCORE.
- Together, we started the Friends of Santa Fe Jazz, producing and bringing national jazz talent to Santa Fe.
- Volunteered at the Georgia O'Keeffe Museum
- Cofounders of Woody's Place at Sagewood in Phoenix.
- Boston Arts Academy. Papa was founder and I worked on the library.
- Israel Cultural Center at Zionist House in Boston. I worked with Kitty Dukakis there.
- And… a few more things you just might discover on your own!

Noni's Jazz Improvisation

Tonight, you will lead like a *lead sheet* and show your family how you do that thing you do and how they can do it too! You're going to teach your family how to do something you love doing and then, give them the space and love to find a new way of doing it too.

Pick one thing you really really love doing. Is it playing the piano or recorder? Singing songs? Drawing pictures? Baking cookies? Brushing your teeth? Got it? Good! Now, what's your unique way of doing this activity? Do you hold your toothbrush with your toes? Do you sprinkle salt in the chocolate chip cookie batter? Do you tickle the ivories like you tickle your sister?

Now, invite your family into the living room, and show them how you do what you love doing. You can mime it, sing it, dance it, wing it! Then, on the count of three, ask them to do that thing (in their own unique way) too! 1, 2, 3…Brush, tickle, sprinkle!

Noni's B-sides

There's an A-side and a B-side to every record. The A-side holds the song that will be released into the world with enough fanfare to make it fly. The B-side, otherwise known as the "flip-side", is considered by some to be less extraordinary than its counterpart, somehow secondary, which is odd because everyone knows that the most compelling music, people, ideas and experiences are always less obvious. Here are some of my B-sides, those little moments that made me who I am, those less obvious gems that have taught me how to fly.

I learned how to dance from Martha Graham. As a youngster I loved dancing, all the time, anywhere, even in the kitchen! So, when I found out that modern dance was being offered at Connecticut College for women…I jumped (or rather, jetéd) at the chance. The teachers of this dance class were none other than Martha Graham and Jose Limon! Two of the most well-known dancers and choreographers of our time, two people who had transformed modern dance as we know it, were teaching me how to dance…it was sheer bliss! I remember Martha Graham starting class by drumming on this gigantic drum, trying to find the beat, define the rhythm for our dance, for our class.

I think that's one reason I love Tai Chi so much. It's slow motions, quiet rhythms, as if moving through water, swimming through sand, Tai Chi is thoughtful of movement in the same, resonant way Martha Graham began class.

Standing up is my jam. I learned this about myself early on when I found myself riding a bike, walking or simply preferring to be upright rather than sitting down. In college, I studied on my bed or in the library or standing at study carols, never at a desk. When I talk on the phone, type on the computer, read or write, I'm usually standing. In fact, I'm at my best when I'm standing 6 to 10 hours a day. Sometimes, I even eat standing up!

Save the bags! This is not a political movement, just a little something you might not know about me. I collect bags. I save bags. Paper bags, cloth bags, vinyl bags, sacs, handbags, and suitcases. I love bags. You might call me a real bag lady! But don't be fooled, I love ribbons, bows and wrapping paper too. On some occasions, I've been known to save paperclips and rubber bands. But back to my first love, bags. I love packing my suitcase, unpacking my suitcase and making it empty and ready for the next adventure. An empty bag is like an open door, full of possibilities. Leaving is always an adventure. Whether it's just across the street or across oceans, I learn by doing, seeing and being. My love of saving bags reminds me of the song "My Favorite Things" from the Sound of Music.

When the dog bites
When the bee stings
When I'm feeling sad
I simply remember my favorite things
And then I don't feel so bad!

Papa and I are film stars. Once, we bid on the "making of a movie of your life," by Emmy Award-winning director, Diana Taylor. We won the prize. Diana brought a soundman and editor to the house. We spent 12 hours making a movie of our life. We changed clothes to make it seem like it was taking place over days. The crew interviewed our friends, three couples: The Hootkins, Tullys and Mikkelsens who spoke about us. With the camera on us, we looked at photographs from our past as they asked about our lives, work and family. We even had to 'take five' which is both film and jazz speak for taking a break. When you kids want to take a break and watch the video, let us know!

Hi! I'm Susanna, I'll be your social director on the cruise ship. I used to watch the TV show *Gale Storm*, a sitcom about life on a cruise ship. Originally, the show had been titled *Oh, Susanna* because the lead character was a cruise director named Susanna Pomeroy (Storm). Because of my name, and love of cruise ships, connecting people and organizing events, I thought that being a social director on a cruise ship would be fantastic! And, in a way, I did end up being a social director, it was just on land instead of at sea.

Nancy's mysterious letter. Because I'm curious by nature, a little bit nosey and I like solving mysterious, there was a time I wanted to be a detective just like Nancy Drew.

In High School, I was in the Majorettes because I didn't make the cheer squad. I could never do a cartwheel, the splits or jump high enough off the ground. But that's ok because I became a majorette! The majorettes were part of the marching band and the band's director was the great, Mr. Benvenutti! I even took private piano lessons from him after school. As a Majorette I learned the art of twirling a baton, hurling it into the air and catching it without missing a beat. I wore white leather boots with tassels and a cute uniform in green and gold silk. Green and gold were the colors of New London High School.

My closet is my palette, stuffed to the brim with colorful clothes and accessories worn throughout the years. It's my palette. If you go to any painter's studio, you'll find that they have tubes and tubes of paint, more colors than you can imagine. Over years of painting their palette has that wonderful crud on it, a patina of pigments, residue of used colors, that's what they need in order to create. Crusty colors that have blended together to form new ones. My palette is a stuffed, overflowing closet with vintage things that are over 50 years old as well as brand-new things from designers and even clothes from Walgreens! I pull things out, put them together and, voila, I'm wearing my art. People say you have to thin out your closet, throw out your closet clutter, get rid of something old every time you buy something new, but I can't, it's part of my creative process. I'm not a hoarder, I'm just an artist with a full palette.

Recently, I read an article in The Wall Street Journal that explicitly stated, "Pink is in," and guess what? I don't need to buy a thing, because I already have pink! And every other color that will surely make a comeback soon. So, I say, Come back shoulder pads, bellbottoms, periwinkle and culottes…I'm ready for you!

We left you a trail of less obvious gems. Eventually, you'll find out that Papa and I left you money for a few of our favorite things: visiting the national parks, Israel and Berklee College of Music. Our hope is that while traveling to (and inhabiting) these places that shaped us, you will take the time to breathe them in and find the less obvious gems between the trees, the sea, the buildings, and the stanzas. Our hope is that you'll find your own small moments that, when added up, become the runway by which you take flight.

All That Jazz

"Come on babe, why don't we paint the town, and all that Jazz" –All That Jazz

"You never see anyone toe-tap to a painting." –Lee Berk

Museums have long been filled with pleasure and treasures for me. These temples dedicated to education and aesthetics have always inspired me, filled me with more questions and answers than could be contained in a single gallery space. I'm drawn to the visual arts: abstracts, the colors, ideas. I'm attracted to the modernism period. At one point, I had a large library filled with art books, which I donated to the Georgia O'Keeffe Museum in Santa Fe. The books are now in their Research Library. I hope you'll go to Santa Fe and visit the books sometime, like visiting a friend you miss, or a song you long to hear. Just walk into the Research Center and politely ask, "May I see the Susan Berk books, please?" When they bring out the books and you're looking at them, carefully peeling each page back, I hope you'll feel like you are visiting me too.

Fashion is another form of visual art. Fashion is a place for dancing. Fashion is a place for playing. The clothes, the colors, the textures, the way they move, the design, it all inspires me. The creativity by the artists and designers; they make masterpieces to be worn. They inspire us to match our hair with their innovations, our makeup and moods to their materials. I love wearable art.

Architecture is also art. I've lived in many beautiful houses. Brick houses, wood houses, houses on golf courses, two-story houses, three-story houses, one-story houses, lofts, and apartments. I've always made these houses into homes no matter how small or grand, they each had their own personality, their own point of view, inspiring me to design spaces inside the homes just as unique as the outsides. Inside our homes, I surrounded myself with my favorite things: china, placemats, napkins, plates, dishes, cups, saucers. I always had a few unique objects so that when I looked at them or used them, they made me feel happy.

Although I love visual art, fashion, and architecture, music is my reason for being, it's a place where my mind can roam, where it's stimulated, where lights dance in different sections of my brain, illuminating my imagination. Like Papa says, "I never saw anyone tapping their toe to a painting." Music moves me. Music is moving. Music moves people to stand up, to dance, to sway, to sing, to clap, to smile, to cry. Music is a vessel for fashion, visual art and architecture; it wraps itself around all other art forms and lifts them up. It's almost like therapy to me. That's what artfulness is, it's an exchange: art for emotions. It's how we engage with objects and materials; how we tap our toes and bring a space to life.

Musical Notes: 2

In one of your grandmother's recordings I can hear what sounds like a metronome in the background. In other recordings, I can hear a fountain or some sort of water feature. Sometimes she tells me the same story, like a refrain, and just when I think I've already heard that story she adds a missing detail. A two-piece velvet dress becomes green and attached by a silver belt. Arturo Sandoval leaves Cuba for Miami in one version of the story and in the next we find out that Dizzy Gillespie was his mentor. She repeats the story until all the beautiful details are there for us to see. She fills in the blanks with songs, "Let's be sure to include In A Sentimental Mood." "Do we have Two For The Road?" "Don't forget to include Our Love is Here to Stay."

Jazz Splits

Next time you find yourself jazz dancing (and feeling adventurous) you can try something called the jazz split. A split, as you may know, is when something breaks into pieces. The jazz split is when you're dancing and your right leg breaks apart from your left leg—don't worry, not literally—and you fall to the floor with your left leg outstretched, your right leg bent at the knee and a smile on your face because you accomplished a really difficult dance move! Sometimes my brain does the jazz split without my permission leaving my thoughts on the floor in front of me, and my brain left behind. These moments when my thoughts split from my brain are called, bipolar episodes.

Maybe you've heard the word episodes before, from TV? Episodes are the small, individual parts that make up the one, larger series. In music, an episode is a smaller passage that isn't really a part of the main composition, but adds a flourish, something unique and necessary, like the sorbet in between courses. During a big, fancy meal, you just might see a small bowl of sorbet placed in front of you, right before the main course is served. The sorbet is used to cleanse your palate, to clear the memory of your mouth's prior bite in order to prepare your taste buds for the main course! So, even though it's part of the meal, it's a slight departure as well (dessert before the main course, preposterous, well...).

Then, of course, there's the medical definition of a bipolar episode, which is described as: *Bipolar disorder, also known as manic-depressive illness, is a brain disorder that causes unusual shifts in mood, energy, activity levels, and the ability to carry out day-to-day tasks. These moods range from periods of extremely "up," elated, and energized behavior (known as manic episodes) to very sad, "down," or hopeless periods (known as depressive episodes). One might experience hearing voices and hallucinations.*

So, what do ALL of these episodes have in common? Although seemingly small and a little off course, all of them have significant impact on the journey. The journey of a meal, a song, a story, a life.

I've had six episodes in my life and these episodes were of the prolonged illness kind. In 1981, after the birth of your mother (and aunt), Lucy, I was diagnosed with bipolar disorder by Dr. Edward Messner a revered psychiatrist affiliated with Massachusetts General hospital.

Now, the thing about me is that I'm prone to worrying, which is a sign of bipolar disorder and these episodes act as an amplifier for worrying. One thing I always worry about is breaking things. I used to worry about technology and fear that if I turned computers and phones on or off too many times I would use up the battery or worse, break them altogether, so I just gave up on using them for a while. As a youngster, another byproduct of worrying was biting my fingernails. My mother was also a worrier whose woes worked their way into her picking at her toenails. So, you can imagine that a diagnosis that left me with broken thoughts was something really big to worry about. Let's just say that there aren't enough fingernails in the world to bite that will quell the worrying of being diagnosed with bipolar disorder.

Prior to being diagnosed, I had an episode where I heard voices in my head. My brain started imagining horrible things. Can you imagine your brain imaging horrible things all by itself? Without your permission? Can you imagine feeling paranoid and trapped in your own head? I desperately wanted to turn the channel, switch to another series and escape my mind. It felt like elephants were stomping on my brain, tromping through my thoughts, a stampede impeding reality. My breathing was labored as thoughts rushed through my mind, gushing with bad feelings.

I want to share this with you, my history of my bipolar disorder episodes because they are part of my longer series, and even though the episodes are terribly frightening for me and those around me, they are a part of me and those around me, too. I've been so grateful to have the support of your papa and your mothers through all of the episodes. I want you to know about my bipolar disorder so you know it's ok to talk about it. So you know it's ok to ask for help. So you know it's ok to speak up. So you know that you are loved and supported by your grandparents, parents and friends. So you know you will be ok no matter what is going on in your brain with or without your permission. I want to destigmatize this issue, so please feel free to talk about it with me.

When I was little my parents were in a constant state of making noise. The stereo was always blaring as they rushed around the house in a cyclone of sound. There was no quiet room in our home. As a kid, I was constantly trying to find quiet. I'd go for bike rides, lie on my bed and daydream, take walks, collect chestnuts, anything to quiet cacophony of sounds. When I'm having a bipolar episode it feels like a very loud house, like elephants let loose in my bedroom. In these episodes my brain tells me that the gas stove is leaking; it tells me to gather my children, grab their coats and shoes because we need to leave the house immediately, even if it's the middle of the night. My brain makes me dive deep into the holocaust and the atrocities that were committed there. An episode feels like the opposite of a glow, it feels like gloom. If there was a cup right in front of me and I reached out to touch it, to take a sip of the water, there would be an invisible force field surrounding it, something keeping my hand from touching the glass. It's like being on the outside of yourself looking in. Like you're watching the slow-motion TV show version of your own life.

After being diagnosed with bipolar disorder, I entered psychoanalysis which is a fancy way of saying that I would go to an office (sometimes four times a week) and share my thoughts, feelings and actions with a doctor who was trained to listen to me and make connections between my thoughts, feelings and actions. Because my brain was imagining horrible things on its own, I was put on a heavy regime of medicines, they called it a "cocktail" but it wasn't fun or fruity, nor did it ever have a maraschino cherry on it. In fact, just the names of medications were hard to choke down: Lithium, Depakote, Klonopin, Zyprexa, Haldol, Ativan, beta-blockers and more medications that I can't even remember the names of. This cocktail made me wheezy, drowsy and sleepy. Like the seven dwarfs only I didn't feel animated or adorable. These side effects meant that when I went to the movies, almost immediately, I'd fall asleep. When driving a car, I couldn't keep my eyes open. This mixture of toxic chemicals also caused a bad tremor in my hands. Picking up a teacup always ended in hot tea erupting from the cup, spraying my clothing, the table, the floor. Writing legibly was never an option with this tremor.

After learning the nuances of this new diagnosis, I started to do very well, in fact, I was doing so well that my doctor took me off all medications. With a clear mind and no episodes in sight, I headed to London on a business trip while Papa stayed at home in Boston.

I went to London to sell Boston. Allow me to explain. I was with tourism professionals and hoteliers to "sell Boston" to Britain as a destination for travelers from the UK. It was called a "Fam Trip" which is a quick trip to familiarize delegates from the convention and visitor's bureau of Boston with those delegates from the convention and visitor's bureau in London. This was a way to create a bridge between both cities. We were meeting to jointly promote Boston and Uncommon Boston and help organize unique tours for visitors from the UK to Boston.

Upon arriving in London, I checked into the London Marriott Hotel at Grosvenor Square along with Ellen the marketing executive from the Marriott Copley. At midnight, I left my hotel room because my brain was starting to do a jazz split and imagine bad things all by itself. I heard voices from the room next door telling me to leave, urging me to get up and get out of the room. I hit the streets looking for your papa, Lee. I was flipping out. I thought he was coming to meet me and he would be arriving at any moment, I just didn't know where. So, I went to the Canadian Embassy (not sure why) and they gave me some money because I had no money with me. I found a taxicab that took me from hotel to hotel to hotel looking for Papa. At each hotel, I booked a room with my credit card because I thought that Papa was going to join me there. I finally ended up in a hotel, I don't remember the name of it, but I was so frightened that I slept in the hallway, outside my room.

When I woke up I went shopping. Wait, before I went shopping I got my haircut really really really short. Then I took off my sweater and slacks and shoes and went shopping. For some reason, I had the strong desire to buy unisex clothing. After shopping, I found a taxi to take me back to the Marriot and meet my friend Deborah Waring, as we had a 10:00am business appointment scheduled. When I arrived at the hotel, with my short short short hair, androgynous clothing and a thick cloud of worry hanging over my head, Deborah knew something was wrong and insisted that I call my family. I said, "No no no no." and insisted on seeing a policeman.

Somehow, a policeman showed up. He looked at me and saw how disoriented I was, how out of shape, out of control, and took me to the police station.

At the police station, I was placed in a cell. I thought I was in Disneyland with Mickey Mouse. This is what happens when your thoughts are in front of you and what you know to be true is bent behind you; strange thoughts become your new reality. Hours later, a doctor who was a psychiatrist, came to evaluate me. She was warm and attentive. She sent me to St. Lukes, which was the oldest psychiatric hospital for the insane in a London suburb. It was closed a few years ago. While in the paddy wagon on the way to St. Lukes, I tried to jump out. It felt like being in a prison cell on wheels, I couldn't take it and needed to leave. Fortunately, I couldn't get out.

Once at the hospital, Papa was called and notified that I was there. He flew to London on the Concord, a very very very fast plane that doesn't exist anymore and cost about $10,000 for a one-way ticket. He arrived within a few hours, rented a little room in a neighborhood near the hospital. I was so scared and paranoid in the hospital, totally convinced that the staff's job was to harm me rather than help me. They put me on heavy medications. Papa visited me every day and when he came to visit we went on walks. I even had my hair washed and set during one of our outings. After about a week in St. Luke's, Papa was given permission from a social worker to bring me home.

That was one of my first episodes. I've had 5 or 6 since then. Usually when traveling away from home, like to New York City, Israel, the Caribbean.

(At this point in the recording, I can hear your grandmother sigh, her mouth moves away from the microphone and then she says: "Um…All this talking about it is very anxiety provoking.")

After the first few episodes, and being placed on a regimen of heavy mediations, I thought I would never laugh again. Do you know what it feels like to not be able to smile? It's as if your entire face feels dull, placid, like all the muscles in your face fell asleep and even when you ask them nicely to wake up and make the corners of your mouth turn upwards, all they can do is resist this request. This was my demeanor for years while my psychiatrist experimented with getting my medication cocktail just right. The result: no laughing, no feeling, and no dreaming. These life-given entitlements, which I had taken for granted, had gone missing and I felt fragile, like a whirling ballerina in a snow globe that had been shaken up and dropped on the ground. The water and snow now seeping out. The globe cracked. The ballerina broken.

But now I feel strong! You've seen me laugh, smile, sing, dance and dream. So, what has brought the change, the transformation to help me feel strong, to laugh from my belly, to dream and enable me to write a memoir? I took a bold step. I committed myself to a psychiatric hospital. I committed myself to McLean Hospital. I was a patient there for about 6 weeks. I gave them my shaky autograph and signed on to a locked ward.

This institution was meant to humanize me—make me feel better—but the tactics felt dehumanizing. No dental floss. *I might slit my wrists.* No mouthwash. *I might get drunk on the alcohol it contained.* No unaccompanied walks. *I might wander off.* There were designated times to make and receive phone calls. Limited pay phones in the hallway shared by many other of residents. Shared laundry facilities where I might find my underwear on the floor if I didn't take it out of the dryer when the buzzer went off. The bed checks; frantic flashlights shining in my face to see if I was sleeping in my bed. The same questions every single morning. "Did you take a shower?" "What is today's date?" "Do you feel like committing suicide?"

They stripped me of all my meds—cold turkey—off the cocktail. They re-diagnosed me more specifically as schizo-affective bipolar and put me on another medication.

I began writing. I wrote to cope with my circumstances and surroundings. The writing brought self-discovery, self-reliance, compassion, understanding. However, no one could experience or see, or hear, what I was seeing, hearing, and feeling. I began journaling, recording daily sessions, describing them. Meds continued to make my hands shaky. I couldn't write on lined paper. I couldn't read my writing. In fact, years hence I would throw out my journals (years of describing dreams, symptoms, actions, and feelings) because I simply couldn't read the garble. The message in the bottle had disappeared like invisible ink. Looking at these journals were painful reminders of loose ends.

Who do I tell? Who do I share my condition with? Like diabetes, I would never be rid of it. The sentence was out. I joined the club of manic-depressives, those with mental disorders, the possible path to future incarcerations, more meds that would make me feel drugged, blood tests to monitor possible organ dysfunctions – trial and error. Fear, stigma, more racing thoughts - I can't wait to get out of here. My life would never be the same.

I am telling you about this time in my life because I survived. Eventually, I left the institution better equipped to deal with this disease, the cocktail was refined and is always being fine-tuned with the help of great doctors. I am surviving the best way I know how by laughing, singing, dancing and dreaming with you. If my brain ever does the jazz split again, it's ok because I have the support and love of all of you (and amazing doctors) and my life is worth living, bipolar and all!

Musical Notes: 3

Tania here, wanting you to know that when your grandmother and I started this project, she told me how important it is for people to know about her bipolar disorder because so many people don't talk about it, because it's stigmatized to the point of people hiding it and sometimes even losing or taking their own lives as a result of this stigma. She wants you to know it's ok to talk about things that might be uncomfortable for you to talk about. It's not always comfortable for your Noni to share these moments with me, but she knows that in the sharing she is helping herself and helping others heal. One very important thing to note about your Noni: Her condition is triggered by some of her favorite activities in life, like traveling. But she never stops traveling. She loves traveling. She also never stops taking her medication. She knows how important it is in stabilizing her condition. Sometimes when she's on a jazz cruise, doing her favorite activity, listening to music for hours and hours, fully immersed in the rhythms and lyrics, she starts to feel sick, like worse than eating 6-gallons of ice cream, sick. Sometimes even jazz music, one of her very favorite things in life, triggers an episode for her, but she never stops listening. Your Noni is brave and sensitive and a really great listener.

Jazz Hands

"The memory of things gone is important to a jazz musician." –Louis Armstrong

On a jazz cruise, jazz, historian and radio scholar, Dick Golden gave a lecture that Papa and I attended a few years ago. During his lecture, he spoke about his friend Tony Bennett. Afterwards, I approached Dick and told him Papa and I have one of Tony Bennett's paintings hanging on our bedroom wall. I told him how we look at the painting every single day. We wake up to it and see it every night before we go to bed. Dick told us that he speaks to Tony every single day. Tony is 90 years old. Dick said that when he told Tony he was getting ready to go on a cruise and probably wouldn't have the best cell phone reception, Tony said, "What am I gonna do when you're on the ship and we can't talk?" I said to Dick, "Want to use my cell phone to call Tony?" He thanked me, but said it wasn't necessary. During the cruise Dick was able to speak to Tony and he mentioned Papa and me to Tony! Do you know what Tony Bennett said? He said he had fond memories of receiving His honorary doctorate in 1974 from Larry Berk Your great grandfather and founder of Berklee.

"It sounds so simple, but if you just be yourself, you're different than anyone else." –Tony Bennett

During his lecture, Dick told a story about author and historian David McCullough who had told him that he once shook the great Louis Armstrong's hand. According to McCullough, that single gesture was one of the most significant moment of his entire life. When I heard that, I started thinking, Papa must have shaken the hands of 50 of the world's most famous people in music, maybe even a 100! From 1979 to 2004, while Papa was the President of Berklee, he awarded many honorary doctorates to musicians, shaking hands with George Benson, David Bowie, Sting, Al Jarreau, Jennifer Holliday, James Taylor, Carly Simon, Steven Tyler, Cleo Laine, Herb Alpert, Steely Dan, Billy Taylor, Phil Collins, Quincy Jones and on and on. Papa's hands have been anointed by the hands of jazz greats, the hands of musicians who have lived up to the Berklee College of Music's motto *Esse quam videri*, which means, "to be, rather than to appear to be."

When Papa retired, both Quincy Jones and Marylin Bergman (among others) sent him handwritten notes. They each wrote about Papa's leadership at Berklee, how kind he was and how he touched so many people, offering them a hand in their careers and their lives. Just by being his unique and talented self, Papa has had the opportunity to shake the hands of great people.

Cool Cats

In jazz lingo (that's right jazz is so cool it's got its own language), "cool cats" refer to those human beings who seem to have been born laid-back. These cats have talents they couldn't hide even if they tried. Cool cats are the people you are drawn to, want to be around, listen to and learn from. Cool cats don't need to act, they just need to be. Cool cats are individuals all the way. I've met a lot of cool cats in my time and continue to meet cool cats all the time. One of my favorite cool cats is Arturo Sandoval. This cat is so cool he's a 10-time Grammy Award winner, a 6-time Billboard Award winner, he won the 2013 Presidential Medal of Freedom, he was founding member of the Grammy Award-winning group Irakere, he's won Emmys, is the protégé of the legendary jazz master, Dizzy Gillespie, AND he's a nice guy! He is robust, energetic and, well…very handsome (it's ok, I told Papa!). But the best part: he's our friend.

Papa and I met Arturo in 2015 on the Entertainment Cruise Production's, Mainstream Jazz Cruise. Now, I had seen Arturo and his wife, Marianela walking the Grand Deck every morning from the first day we had arrived on the cruise. I saw them there because I was walking too. Now, before you ask, "Noni! Did you talk to him?" Let me tell you this: walking, for me, is a place of deep thought, of exercise and meditation; it's a time when my mind and body are working in chorus, so I didn't want to be a drag, which is jazz lingo for "bring someone down," and interrupt his thoughts, exercise and mind/body connection. Don't worry, though, we did meet him.

Now, sometimes people are brought together by happy occasions, like weddings, births, Bar/Bat Mitzvahs, album release parties; and sometimes people are brought together by occasions that are unexpected and have deep sadness attached to them. Arturo and I were brought together by the latter. Shortly after the cruise, one of Arturo's band members jumped off a rooftop and ended his life. It's not easy to tell you this, but you know that your Noni isn't someone to shy away from subjects that aren't easy. I'm telling you because when we talk about subjects that aren't easy to talk about; they become easier to talk about. Having recently been an Executive Producer on a documentary film by Lisa Klein and Doug Blush called *The S Word* about suicide (I'll tell you more about the film and my involvement later), I had empathy for Arturo and his friend. I wrote Arturo a note, expressing our sympathies. He wrote Papa and me back in response to his bandmate's suicide saying, "I can't get it out of my head." I introduced Arturo to Lisa, the filmmaker of *The S Word* and Arturo donated his music (in the form of CDs) to the film's Kickstarter campaign so they could give away CD's as a gift to those who donated to the film.

When Arturo came to perform at the Scottsdale Center for the Performing Arts, we saw our chance to really connect with him, so we invited him to lunch. He graciously accepted and we whisked him away to T. Cook's in the Royal Palms. What a charming man. We spent several hours together talking about music and relationships and ideas. He said two powerful things during that lunch that I will never forget and I want to share with you, "Music is the balm of the soul." And "Music heals the spirit." As someone who lives with bipolar disorder, I too believe that music sooths the soul.

Over lunch, Arturo shared with us stories about his life in Cuba; how he was born near Havana in November of 1949. How he struggled emotionally while in Cuba because the only thing he loved doing, playing jazz, was illegal. Can you imagine if drawing, dancing, playing piano was illegal? At the age of 40, his mentor, Dizzy Gillespie, helped him leave Cuba. He ended up settling in Miami because that's where his parents were living. Eventually, his parents passed away, which paved the way for him and his wife to leave Miami and head to Los Angeles. Arturo appreciates the freedom he found in the United States. If you ever want to learn more about Arturo and his harrowing life, there is a film called *For Love or Country*. The famous actor Andy Garcia plays Arturo.

A good way to connect with good friends is to find out what you have in common. It turns out that Arturo, Marianela, Papa and I have A LOT in common! Arturo met his wife the same year I met Papa, 1975. I met Papa in May and Arturo met Marianela in July. Both of us couples were married in October. Papa and me after 5 months of courtship, Arturo and Marianela after 3 months. We each have 2 children. Their son was born in 1976 the same year that Nancy was born. Arturo is a real family man and when he's not touring, he sees his granddaughter as much possible. He and his wife love babysitting their granddaughter. His daughter-in-law is Arturo's music manager. His love and commitment to his family deeply resonates with Papa and me.

Arturo Sandoval is known as one of the most dynamic and vivacious live performers of our time. He has been seen by millions of people, can deftly play classical, jazz, rock and traditional Cuban music. He's played with all the great symphonies, he's an amazing composer, plays trumpet, keyboard and even sings, but most of all he is an endearing and enduring friend. He causes a sensation wherever he entertains, even if it's at lunch!

Another cool cat was the music icon, Prince. A few years ago, Prince was giving a concert in Boston. The Berklee students at the time raced to Tower Records on the corner of Newbury Street and Mass Avenue in hopes of purchasing a ticket for Prince's concert later that night. As the students and other Prince fans stood in line, a car came racing down Mass Avenue, jumped the median and drove directly into the crowd of Prince fans waiting to purchase tickets. One of our students was struck by the car and killed. When Prince learned of this horrific accident, he decided to dedicate all the proceeds from that evening's concert to a scholarship in memory of that student at Berklee College of Music.

George Benson is one of the most famous jazz guitarists and vocalists ever. In the summer of 2015, I listened to his album *Givin' It Up* over and over again. I listened to it every single day while walking along the boardwalk in Coronado. The music created a score for my morning walks and was too delicious to stop listening to so I had to give it up and lean into that album all summer long!

At some point, George Benson made his way to Scottsdale, Arizona. One afternoon, he came to hear the Joey DeFrancesco concert at Sagewood that Papa was producing. After the concert, George came up to the front row and started kibitzing with Papa and me and I said, "George would you like to stay for dinner?" And he said, "Oh no, not dinner, but I'll have a glass of wine." Well, we all adjourned to the Mesquite Grill and that glass of wine turned into a two-hour long conversation over pizza and wine.

We sat in the bar area. It was Papa, me, George, the drummer, Janell and our friends from the jazz cruises, Paul and Sue Lowden. We served wine and iced water and ordered three or four pizzas. The pizza George loved the best was the one with smoked barbeque chicken. George told us about his life growing up in Pittsburgh. How as a kid he would sell newspapers on the corner for a quarter or a five-cent piece. One day, someone gave him a broken-down ukulele. George fixed it up and started to play on the street corners and, pretty soon, people would throw coins to the boy who was playing so well. He made more money playing music than he ever did selling newspapers! That was the beginning of his entire career as a guitar player and singer-songwriter. He became an outstanding guitarist and mentor to aspiring musicians. Papa gave him an honorary doctorate from Berklee in 1990.

Gary Burton is a Grammy-winning jazz vibraphonist and composer who has played with the Harlem String Quartet, bridging jazz and classical music together beautifully. His book "Learning to Listen" is one of the best books I've ever read. It's about learning to listen to himself as a musician, coming out as a gay man and, of course, listening to the music, allowing it to guide you rather than the other way around.

He was a preacher's son from Indiana who went to Berklee to pursue music. He left Berklee to be with his musical mentor, the great saxophonist Stan Getz. Gary writes music and plays the vibraphone with four mallets at the same time, it's astounding to watch and even more impressive to listen to. He's a big collaborator and delights in moving in and out of genres, sometimes playing with his good friends Chick Corea and Makoto Ozone. Both his music and friendships are enduring. He has a radio show, teaches classes online, and is multifaceted and multidimensional. As well as being a great friend and a cool cat!

Noni's Jazz Improvisation

Do you know any cool cats? Anyone who stands out in crowd? Who's more of a circle than square? Are you a cool cat? Next time you see a cool cat or you're feeling like a cool cat, I want you to snap your fingers twice and in your mind, say, "Being a cool cat is where it's at!" Heck, if you're feeling extra cool, you can say it out loud. Being a cool cat is where it's at!

Magical Musical Journey

"Yesterday is history, tomorrow is a mystery, today is God's gift, that's why we call it the present."—Joan Rivers

"Music is magic, magic is life." —Jimmy Hendrix

"Roll up and that's an invitation, roll up for the mystery tour.
Roll up to make a reservation, roll up for the mystery tour.
The magical mystery tour is waiting to take you away,
Waiting to take you away." –The Beatles (Magical Mystery Tour)

When I was a sophomore in high school I read a book that changed my life forever called, *Junior Year Abroad*. The book was about a young girl who spends her junior year in Paris. The story was one of romance, travel and fashion, effervescence, excitement, beauty and adventure. This book was the kindling that lit the fire in me to spend time abroad.

When I was in high school I only wanted to go to a college that had a travel abroad program. So you can imagine my excitement when I found one at Beaver College, which is now Arcadia University. Back then it was a women's college located in Glenside, PA, just outside of Philadelphia. In 1965, Beaver had one of the first international study abroad programs. Now it has one of the largest and most celebrated programs attracting students from many elite colleges and universities throughout the world.

When it came time to choose my travel abroad destination, the most natural and easy choice for me was London, England. We had family-friends in England, Jerry and Dorothy Waring. My mother and father had met the Warings while vacationing in Paris. And, because I was born in New London, I just knew that old London had to be even more charming! During the second semester of my Junior year at Beaver, I hopped the pond and landed in London.

Our advisor and chaperone for the trip was Dr. Hazard the magical, pied piper of our entire England experience. He believed that we should see the places we were reading about in books. He brought school to life. We studied Welsh in Wales, architecture in Canterbury, art in the British Museum. When we were studying Robin Hood he took us to Nottingham Forest! The Old Vic Theatre became our regular stomping grounds. Hampstead Heath, Kew Gardens, the Chelsea flower show and the Royal Academy became our classrooms. My education was royal. I attended classes at the City of London College and even skipped some classes in favor of directly experiencing this magical mystery land.

This amazing educational experience took place at the same time The Beatles were on their Magical Mystery Tour. It felt like we were running parallel lives to The Beatles and it was only a matter of time before we would bump into them on Carnaby Street. Carnaby Street was in SoHo, a small, vibrant area in Westminster known for its shopping, wild fashion, cafes, and Lady Jane's the first women's fashion boutique on the street. It's where young people went to see and be seen in the 60's. Many musicians wrote songs about Carnaby Street like The Kinks, The Jam, Peggy March and more. You didn't run down Carnaby Street, you promenaded.

I promenaded in my Carnaby best, which was a neon emerald green miniskirt with black piping on the sides and white knee-high boots. When I was feeling a bit more conservative, I wore a tailored wool suit with a brightly colored floral print silk scarf neatly tied around my neck. We called these scarves "liberty scarves" because we bought them at the Liberty department store. I still love bouncing around from Brooks Brothers preppy to way-out designers, it's in my nature to explore.

I lived in a townhouse in Egerton Gardens in South Kensington, near the Victorian Albert Museum. I was either walking everywhere or taking the Tube (the subway). When I first arrived at the townhouse where I would be staying, I had a very warm welcome! There was a Shilling heater in my room, something I had never seen before, and as I brushed passed it in my brand new green velveteen, floor-length bathrobe, I smelled something odd and quickly realized that my bathrobe was on fire! When I wrote home, I made a joke of it and said, "I had a very WARM welcome to London. Very warm indeed!"

As much as I was learning from school, I was learning more from the school of life. We visited Yad Vashem in Israel, the memorial to the Holocaust. I was deeply moved by this. I learned so much about my roots as a student in London, because during spring break trips I traveled to Germany, Poland and Russia. In Germany, I found my way to the Dachau concentration camp and in Russia I visited the Grande synagogue in Moscow all by myself. I was introduced to opera, theater, museums, and travel on a grand scale. I saved my bi-weekly allowance that I was supposed to spend on food and spent much of it on admissions to museums and theater tickets. Every morning I stuffed myself on the breakfast provided for us in the boarding house so I wouldn't have to waste money on food. Sugared cornflakes, broiled tomatoes, 2 sunny side eggs with bacon, toast, butter, jam, milk and tea or coffee, then I would leave for the day and only return home when it was dark and I was sufficiently stuffed on arts and culture.

When I returned to Beaver, I worked the front desk of the Thomas dormitory for Mrs. Huntoon, the dorm mother. My job consisted of reading the New York Times cover to cover while waiting for girls to sign in and out of the dorm before curfew. Although I longed to be back in London, Beaver was equally mystical and magical, in fact, there was a real castle on campus with turrets, velvet walls, gargoyles and gilded moldings built by Italian craftsman. There were plenty of stories to learn and adventures to have on campus. It didn't matter where I was in the world, to me, life has always felt like a journey, a never ending magical mystery tour.

Musical Couples

There's something about jazz that attracts good people to it. It beckons those who possess a playful spirit, who live life to the fullest, and are open to improvisation at every turn. Jazz seems to assemble a family everywhere it goes. The music is always enduring and deep, reflecting emotions and stories about human pathos and joy and hard times. Jazz has a way of making you go to the places that feel uncomfortable, it guides you to go deeper inside yourself, to stretch yourself. It challenges us to be in a constant state of flux, shifting gears between leading and following, listening and playing, giving and receiving. In return, it asks us to collaborate more, to listen more, to trust more. This is why I love Jazz.

Papa and I are jazz gypsies now, we follow musicians to all four corners of the world. We've come across some compelling couples on our jazz journeys who became fast friends, like Joyce and George Wein. George's parents wanted him to be a doctor, but he ended up being the most famous jazz impresario instead. Eventually he received an honorary doctorate from Berklee. It just goes to show you that there's more than one way to become a doctor! He was the founder of the Newport Jazz Festival in Rhode Island and Storyville in Boston, as well as co-founder of the Newport Folk Festival with the great Pete Seeger.

George is a great pianist and author of "Myself Among Others: A Life in Music". George met his wife, Joyce when she was a student at Simmons College studying social work. They ended up getting married in 1959. Joyce is African American, which is important to the story because in 1959 for a white, Jewish guy to marry a black woman was avant-garde. The word avant-garde means: new and unusual or experimental ideas in the arts. So, it was fitting that Joyce and George, with their love of jazz and each other, fit so well together.

Recently, we saw George on the jazz cruise, by this time Joyce had passed away. He was still talking about Joyce as if she were with us. In jazz when someone dies it's not over, just like when a song finishes, you can always play it again. The memories and music endure even when someone has passed away. When Papa and I are gone, you can read this book again and again and then we are alive.

Larry and Alma formed a loving and musical partnership. This musical couple made Papa, Berklee and made me feel very welcomed into the family. Alma and Larry were Papa's parents and my parents-in-law. They passed away within three weeks of each other in 1995. Alma passed away first from dementia and bedsores.

Larry's heart weakened after Alma's passing. We believe he died of a broken heart. The music that played at their memorial included: "Tea for Two" their favorite song, played by pianist Everett Dean Earl, "Amazing Grace," "Overjoyed," "Isn't It Romantic," and the finale was "When You Wish Upon a Star." Larry always played "When You Wish Upon A Star" on his piano, a black Steinway, for Nancy and Lucy. He also played "Over the Rainbow."

Herb Alpert and Lani Hall. Lani wrote a great memoir and Herb set it to music. They have been together for over 40 years and are still going strong. They love their children. Herb is known for the Tijuana Brass and Lani as lead vocalist with Sergio Mendes and Brasil '66. The two came together and have become one of the most beautiful relationships in the musical world. When they perform together you can feel the love, joy and respect they have for one another. Herb is a fabulous contemporary painter and sculptor as well. He has shown us images of his work on his iPhone when we were backstage at the Musical Instrument Museum (MIM) in Phoenix and at his jazz club in Bel Air. They are a healthy couple; happy, in good shape, excited about life. Music continues to bring them together. Music has brought us together as friends.

Cleo Laine and John Dankworth were our buddies when we lived in Boston. They were from the United Kingdom (UK). Cleo has a magnificent voice, her articulation is stunning, especially when singing or reading Shakespeare. Here is another couple that shows us how playing together leads to staying together. Cleo the chanteuse from England singing classical and jazz while John accompanies her on saxophone. Her curly red hair, her style, those designer kaftans from Egypt flowing on her body. She flows. Cleo and John would come to Boston and stay at the Sonesta Hotel on the Charles, where we would all have lunch together and talk about upcoming concerts, places we've traveled to and jazz music. Both received honorary doctorates from Papa at Berklee. We became such good friends that Cleo invited us to one of her big birthday celebrations held at Town Hall in New York City. Among the guests was Princess Margaret. We'll never forget that evening filled with song; what a royal bash! John has since passed away and Cleo is aging in England not far from London, near the Old Rectory, Wavendon, Milfin Keynes. I miss them terribly. The four of us shared so much.

Arif and Latife Mardin from Turkey are no longer with us, but we cherish the memories we shared with them. Arif received a scholarship to attend Berklee from your great-grandfather, Lawrence Berk. Arif came all the way from Turkey to study in Boston and quickly rose through the ranks of the music world to become a famous producer working with Ahmet Ertegun at Atlantic Records. Arif received the Lifetime Achievement

Award from the Grammy's. He produced Bette Midler, Barbara Streisand, Queen Latifah, Nora Jones, and so many more. Arif and Latife were a warm, loving couple with three beautiful children: Joe, Julie and Nazan.

One memory I cherish was when Bette Midler was singing "Wind Beneath My Wings" at Afri's birthday party. Another was the memorial that Joe organized at the Avery Fisher Hall in the Lincoln Center to remember and celebrate Arif's life. A documentary was made about Arif called *The Greatest Ears in Town: The Arif Mardin Story*. We miss him and his ears. We loved this musical couple very much.

Mike and Cilla Gibbs are another famous couple that we adored. Mike composed the music that was played during my first date with Papa. You could say that Mike composed the music that helped Papa and me fall in love. Mike was from Rhodesia and Cilla from London. He was both a student and faculty member at Berklee. Cilla passed away from cancer. They had two daughters. One passed away, the other daughter lives with Mike in Spain along with his grandchild. Mike wrote and directed *The Only Chrome Waterfall Orchestra*. This was the album playing when I fell in love with Papa at a Berklee College concert, while Papa's parents Alma and Larry were sitting behind us. Mike's songs underscored our first date. Listening to his music made me feel joyful, happy, and sexy. Mike recently met up with us while we were in Spain vising Berklee in Valencia. In October, 2017, we met in Boston to relive our first date and honor Mike, the now famous composer, with a Berklee doctorate.

Paul and Linda McCartney. Like Cilla, Linda McCartney passed away from cancer. Linda was the kind of photographer that captured the spirit of her subjects with a click of the camera. She was a fabulous photographer. I have an autographed copy of her book, *Linda McCartney's Sixties: Portrait of an Era*. Jimmy Hendrix is on the cover and it's filled with images of rock bands. Of course, Paul was a member of one of the most well-known bands of our lifetimes, The Beatles, but the way we met Paul was in Liverpool, England during an official opening of the LIPA (Liverpool Institute of Performing Arts). The LIPA building had once been a school where Paul and some of the other Beatles went as kids. The building was redesigned and turned into a beautiful college, which I'm sure Paul is very proud of. Papa and I were at the opening of LIPA, enjoying the vegetarian food that was provided by Linda's catering company, and then Paul stood up to make remarks. He gave a speech about how he wished his father had been there to be part of this celebration, to see the reopening of his school as a larger arts institute.

I've heard people make this kind of statement before, a moment when they recognize their father or mother and express how they wish their loved one could be present at the event. The moment Paul expressed this I realized how important it is to be present and celebrate the brilliance, beauty and passion of our family while we are still here. This is the reason why I'm writing my memoir, to share with you, my children, my grandchildren, and future great-grandchildren to learn who Papa and I are as people and how much we love who you are. We love and respect all of your brilliance, beauty and passion and we want to leave you with all of our passion for family, music and arts.

We deeply believe that the act of sharing music helps the spirit grow. Even when there is nothing else left, even if one has Alzheimer's or dementia, music is the last element to leave the memory. That's why music therapists play music for patients lost in their body, because music can make one come alive.

So, to you grandchildren and great-grandchildren to come, I hope you will always have music in your lives. Maybe you'll absorb a little bit of all that jazz these musical couples brought to each other and to the world. Whether it's how your paternal great-grandparents, Larry and Alma Berk founded and built the Berklee College of Music, how Herb and Lani share the stage and play with love, joy and respect, or how your maternal great-grandparents, David and Elaine Ginsberg, loved to dance around the house so much that they rarely turned their stereo off!

<u>Lee Berk, Berk Lee…What's in a Name</u>

(In this photo: Bob Share, Dave Brubeck, Larry Berk)

My husband's name backwards is Berk Lee. When my father-in-law, Lawrence Berk (his given name was Berkowitz but for professional reasons changed it to Berk) started teaching in the early 40's he was a certified music teacher for the Schillinger method. Schillinger was a famous music teacher in New York City that many people like Benny Goodman, George Gershwin, Glen Miller and my father-in-law studied with. The Schillinger method incorporated mathematics and music. Larry had a degree from MIT in architectural engineering and he was a jazz pianist, arranger, and composer at a time when there was no formal educational system for jazz.

In the 1940's my father-in-law moved back to Boston from New York and started teaching the Schillinger method. In 1945 he started his own school called the Schillinger House. After several years, Schillinger had passed away and the school was no longer based on the Schillinger theory. So my father-in-law decided to change the name. He started telling his colleagues and friends that he needed to come up with a new name, and fast! Fred Berman, a trumpet teacher at Schillinger, burst into Larry's office one morning and said, "Larry, I had a dream last night, and you should call the school Berklee. It's your son's name backwards."

The name stuck. Lee was only 5 or 6 years old when they named it.

Lee studied at Brown University where he received a Bachelor of Arts in Political Science and then received a Juris Doctorate from Boston University Law School. After he graduated, his father said, "Lee, I'd like you to come work at Berklee. I need you." Lee started working at his namesake, and became responsible for teaching business courses to musicians. Lee went on to write a book, *Legal Protection for the Musician* which won the ASCAP Deems Taylor Award. Lee wrote another book, a coffee table book, on the history of Berklee. Lee loves writing, he has always loved writing, in fact, he wanted to go to Stanford to study writing.

Lee's tenure as President of Berklee lasted over 25 years. His style of leadership was open; he listened to everybody. When everyone wanted things one way and he wanted them another, he honored the majority. His management style was based on openness, collaboration and integrity.

At one point during his time at Berklee I had an office right next to Lee's. I was doing hospitality for the parents, musicians and students of Berklee so this made sense. But that didn't last too long.
Tania: Why?
Susan: Because we would come home, at night, and continue doing work.
Tania: So, there was no opportunity to connect as a couple?
Susan: Right. And sometimes I'd be annoyed because I hadn't heard about something and got it from a third party, so when I'd get home, I was like, 'Lee, why didn't I know? Why didn't you tell me…' It was too much.
Tania: So, who helped you change it?
Susan: A psychiatrist named Dr. Messner. He said, 'You decided to marry each other and love one another, you didn't decide you were going to work together.' It works for some couples to be business partners. It didn't work for us.

International Jazz Day

"My father took me to a jazz concert, and it wasn't until later in life that I realized: 'Maybe that's why I got really interested in jazz.'"– President Barack Obama

When we first learned about the White House Jazz concert from Karen Scates, I thought of my father-in-law, Lawrence Berk and his wife Alma who had been guests of President Jimmy Carter and Rosalynn Carter for a jazz picnic on the Rose Garden Lawn. Immediately I said to myself, *Wouldn't it be wonderful if Papa and I could have a similar opportunity under President Barack Obama*? So, I contacted the current President of Berklee, Roger Brown to see if there was a way for us to celebrate jazz with the President! Roger happily told us that he would look into it. Well, Roger pulled some strings in the White House and with local senators, and Papa and I (as well as Roger and his wife Linda) were on the list for International Jazz Day concert at

The White House on Friday, April 21, 2016. April is Jazz Appreciation Month and for the past five years, there has been a Jazz Appreciation Day celebrated in countries around the world. This particular year, the host country was the United States and the concert was orchestrated by Herbie Hancock and others. As luck would have it, it was the exact same time period of my Advisory Board meeting for the National Museum of Women in the Arts in Washington, so months earlier I had made hotel reservations at the Sofitel, walking distance from the White House!

We were two of only 500 guests. We were told to be at a specific gate on the side of the White House at 5:00pm and we were permitted to enter at 5:30pm. They gave us no other information except, "business attire." Ooh, the intrigue!

We arrived promptly at 5:00pm and there were already many people lined up including Bill Richardson, the former governor of New Mexico who had appointed Papa as Chairman of the Music Commission for the state. Soon we were invited to step into the White House, but almost as quickly as we stepped, we were stopped and asked for identification. We were permitted to walk a few more feet through the security scanner and…we were inside the White House.

Immediately upon entering the grand space, a student jazz group was playing, setting the tone for the evening. We made our way up to the second floor of the White House, which was filled with people milling about and hors d'oeuvres being passed around the room by smiling young people in white shirts and bowties. We saw former Secretary of State, Madeline Albright. I was excited to meet her, as I had seen her pin collection displayed in a few museums. I struck up a conversation with her by commenting on the three attractive rhinestone jazz pins she was wearing. The night was off to an amazing start.

At 6:30pm we were all ushered back downstairs to the first floor and into a large enclosed tent right there on the White House lawn. It was gigantic, almost as big as the White House itself. Many of the seats inside the tent were reserved for dignitaries including President Obama and First Lady, Michelle. In the tent we spotted Nancy Pelosi, Al Sharpton, Tom Perez, Wolf Blitzer, and Joe Biden.

President Obama opened the evening with remarks about the history and significance of jazz, then the performers took the stage. It was a star-studded evening including Chick Corea, Terri Lyne Carrington, Pat Metheny, Sadao Watanabe, Esperanza Spalding, Daniela Perez, Herbie Hancock, Aretha Franklin, Al Jarreau, and Sting. Many of the musicians had some relationship with Berklee, whether they had been a teacher or student or honorary doctorate degree recipient. This realization was profoundly humbling for Papa and me.

President Obama and First Lady, Michelle closed the evening with gracious remarks and observations about the value of jazz. Papa and I floated out of the White House knowing that we had just experienced a once in a lifetime jazz celebration.

We are truly blessed to know, listen and learn from the movers and shakers of the international jazz movement.

A Family of Presidents

I've always respected leadership and leaders. In grade school when Secretary of State, John Foster Dulles (under Eisenhower) was reported sick and in the hospital, I bought a card that looked like an elephant and asked all my classmates to sign it. The card was sent off to The White House. The White House wrote back and thanked us for our concern! The letter was signed by Dulles himself. I was class secretary for eight years: four in high school and four in college. Although I was never class president, I have been a president (once) and am related to (and love) MANY presidents. Allow me to explain.

Lucy once said, "Ok, Dad you're retiring soon, so maybe I'll come work at the college, become the president, and then they can name the school BerkLucy."

Elaine Miller Ginsberg: President of the New London Public Library and of the South Eastern Connecticut United Way. Elaine died from cancer in September of 1995, at the age 72.

David Ginsberg: President of Rotary Inc. New London. David died from old age in July of 2011 at 91 years old.

Marc Ginsberg: My brother was the president of his golf club and president of the Stonington Public Library.

Susan Berk: President of the New Mexico Committee of Women in the Arts

Lee: President of Berklee College of Music. He also received a special Grammy from the Recording Academy called the "President's Merit Award" for more than 30 years of outstanding educational achievement. The other people that were honored with this award that same year included Van Cliburn, Carol King, and Marian McPartland.

Alma: Founder and Director of Publicity at Berklee College of Music. Alma died from dementia in December of 1995 at the age of 83.

Larry: President of Berklee College of Music. Larry died three weeks after Alma from heart failure at the age of 87.

Noni's Jazz Improvisation

If you're an open, fair and kind leader, chances are pretty good that you will end up being president of something too! What will you be president of? Will you be Class President? President of your school's music club? President of the Board of Directors for an arts organization (like your Noni)? The President of the United States? When you become President of Something and you are asked to host a special, international concert; what kind of music will you have? Will it be jazz? Classical? Rock 'n roll? Hip hop? Or something else? Give me a call and let me know what styles of music you choose when you're President!

Sixteen Hawes Street   Brookline, Mass.

ARTS & CRAFTS STYLE HOUSE   Sotheby's
BROOKLINE, MASSACHUSETTS   INTERNATIONAL REALTY

<u>Home</u>

Home, home on the range,
Where the deer and the antelope play,
Where seldom is heard a discouraging word,
And the skies are not cloudy all day.

56

We sang this song often at home as children and then adults. I played it on the piano and on the guitar; it quieted me, settled me down and made me feel at home no matter where I was. Perhaps this cowboy song prepared me for horseback riding in Tucson, hiking in New Mexico and living in Arizona. Papa always said that if we were back in the covered wagon days I would be right with him in the front seat.

But before I made my way out West, I lived out East in New London, Connecticut. The first house I lived in was on Ocean Avenue, number 1190, built by my grandfather, George Miller and located across from Ocean Beach Park. Ocean Beach Park was famous for being washed away in a hurricane in 1928. It was also well known for its wooden boardwalk, penny arcades, jukeboxes, pinball machines, and skee ball games. I loved playing the games at The Gam, always trying to win a prize, any prize; a stuffed animal, a kazoo. There were food stands, too, filled with cotton candy and clam fritters. The smells of sugar, bubbling oil and the salty ocean still fills my memories.

As teenagers, we hung out at The Gam, a gaming area at Ocean Beach Park. My parents imagined bad things happening there (smoking and gambling) and it soon became off limits to me. Once, I told my parents a tall tale to throw them off my tracks as I slipped away, out of the house and into The Gam to meet up with friends.

Ocean Beach was owned and operated by the city of New London and had an Olympic sized outdoor pool where I learned how to swim and earned my red cross lifesaving badge. Ocean Beach also had fun rides like the Ferris Wheel, merry-go-round, carousel, bumper cars, tilt-a-whirl. I will never forget being on a date wearing a gorgeous long dark brown wig as we spun around in the tilt-a-whirl until my wig literally tilted and whirled off my head. I made a joke of it and told my date, "I fall for you!"

Sometimes I dared to go barefoot on that boardwalk. Sometimes I ended up with splinters stuck deep in my feet for which I had to go to the nurse's station.

Across the street from Ocean Beach was my home; a 2-story red brick home built by my grandparents. Initially, I shared a room with my sister Jane and we only had one upstairs bathroom that the entire family shared. The house had a wonderful screened in porch and a cement backyard with a clothesline that stretched across the yard holding our wet clothes as they tried to dry in the ocean air. We had a barbeque pit, which looked like a fireplace and nearby wooden picnic table. All the houses in the neighborhood were close to one another. Some of the houses housed "summer people," people who only stayed until the weather decided to become cold. This meant that during the winter months it was very quiet in our neighborhood.

The house had a garage that stored our bicycles and as you know the bicycle has always been a big part of my freedom. I used to ride my bike to the beach and just before arriving at the water, I'd rest the bike on its side and walk out onto the rocks and wonder about my life. As the salty water jumped up from the ocean to nip my feet, I thought about my future: Would I get married? What will my life look like? Will I feel free? I would sing and hum "There's a place for me" from West Side Story.

Our next house in New London was located at 11 Admiral Drive, just a block from a private beach by the New London lighthouse. I was about 12 or 13 years old when we moved. My parents built this home. It was brick too. Brick was the fashion. It was a split-level with four bedrooms located up a few stairs. I wanted my parents to purchase an old house with a koi pond and lots of secret hiding places and dramatic staircases. But they opted to buy a piece of land and build this one new. That neighborhood was really nice. Paul Gitlin used to drive me to high school every day. The Solomons were good neighborly friends. I had a small crush on their son, Walt Solomon. Dr. I.A. was an inventor scientist with Pfizer. And there were Rose and Sigmund Strochlitz, who were holocaust survivors. I was friendly with their daughter Romana.

Another house I remember was my first home with your Papa Lee. It was an apartment on the 18th floor. 18J of Prudential, the Gloucester Building. We had a balcony. We could see the Charles River. We spent a lot of time on the balcony. When Nancy was a baby and would cry, I would bring her out to the balcony to get fresh air. She stopped crying almost immediately and fell asleep. Even though it was an elegant apartment (above Lord & Taylor department store and near Saks 5th Avenue) I didn't want to raise a family in an apartment.

So, in 1976, we bought a condominium at 65 Commonwealth Avenue, a couple of blocks from the Ritz-Carlton and Boston Public Garden. The apartment was formerly owned by Sarah Fredericks the Grande dame of fashion who had a shop on Newbury Street and in Palm Beach, Florida. Our neighbor downstairs was Sidney Rabb founder and owner of the Stop and Shop grocery store chain. Another neighbor was George Balentine who worked for Sotheby's. It was a fancy address. Since we had no private parking space, we didn't own a car. We had taxicab vouchers and traveled by taxi with brown and white Boston CAB and black and white Town Taxi for seven years. Across Clarendon Street was the wonderful Clarendon Street Playground of which we were founders. All the neighborhood children loved playing there. Lucy went to school at John

Winthrop nursery school and Nancy went to the Thom Montessori school before both girls enrolled in Buckingham Browne & Nichols in Cambridge, Masachusettes.

Our condo was on the 4th floor, it was 3,000 square feet and decorated with marble fireplaces and crystal chandeliers. An oil painting of a woman in an oval shaped gilded molding hung above the dining room fireplace. Underneath the dining room table was a service bell to call for "staff" and off the kitchen was a beautiful pantry that could house China and crystal for 100. There were two wood paneled dens with linen fold wood that supposedly was taken from a bombed-out library in London. Papa and I shared a partner's desk made out of the same wood. We designed our daughters canopy beds draped with fabric. The back of Lucy's bed was an old hotel desk that had been painted white, pink and blue by a well-known artist.

We each had our own bathrooms and walk-in closets. The living room had an expanse of about 50-feet anchored by a very large, handsome antique wooden breakfront that my parents bought us as a house gift. We think it was from the Netherlands. Curious enough, when we went to move this piece of furniture we discovered the wall had never been painted, instead someone "painted around" the furniture!

As their house gift to us, Lee's parent's bought us a white Yamaha baby grand piano which so many famous people played, like Cyrus Chestnut and Makoto Ozone. I played it too. I took lessons throughout my pregnancy with Lucy. We used our home and piano for birthday parties, tea parties, salons, musicals, and the Friends of Berklee parties. This home was made for entertaining and socializing. At some point, we bought the rear apartment on the same floor and opened it up. We even had room for a live-in babysitter, Leslie McPherson. We made an art room for the girls and had a pool table. It was an exceptional 5,000 square foot home, but with no parking, so the children went to school by school bus. Eventually we had to buy a car.

I wanted to work from home, but one of our neighbors felt that working from a residential building was not appropriate. In the thick of writing a book, managing Uncommon Boston (with a few employees), and juggling client meetings, a neighbor threatened to call a lawyer if I didn't stop running my business from our home. Instead of hiring an attorney or having a fight or giving in, I said we needed to move and Lee agreed with me. We regret that choice to this day. Eventually, I moved my office into a basement apartment in a lovely brick townhouse owned by Al Walker.

Later, however, we moved into a beautiful 3-story Queen Anne, over 100-year-old house on the Longwood Mall in Brookline. Longwood Mall is a historic mall known for its 125-year-old beech trees. In fact, the mall is on the historical preservation trust. Every year the neighborhood would gather and plant daffodils and tulip bulbs around the trees. Our 3rd floor became my workspace. I felt free to work and hire employees who could have their own offices too. We had a few live-in Japanese students from the Katherine Gibbs Secretarial School in Boston. Each girl had her own room.

In that home, Lucy had a four-poster bed set. Nancy had beautiful French provincial furniture. Eventually Lucy moved to the 3rd floor and we made her room a workout space and hired a personal trainer. The home had 7 fireplaces, 7 bathrooms, an eat-in kitchen, a breakfast room with strawberry wallpaper and wooden Spanish dining room set. The formal dining room was wood paneled with a brass chandelier and the furniture in the style of Queen Anne and Chippendale. We purchased a lot of furniture from the former owners John and Betina Lodge; they also owned a house with a ballroom in Nantucket.

We brought our large crystal chandelier from 65th Avenue with us and hung it in the music room. Once again, we entertained, gave parties, and created a house filled with furniture, life, people and music. All the important things. This is the home where we celebrated Papa's 50th birthday by hosting a beautiful party for him with 50 guests. Our house was on a corner lot so when the wind would blow, all the leaves from the beech trees would fly into our yard. I was constantly raking and bagging, bagging and raking.

During this same time, we purchased a home in Woodstock, Vermont. One day, Lee went to Woodstock to check out a historic home that he had seen advertised in the Wall Street Journal. He came back with a gift for me: a 250-year-old home. I loved it. It was white clapboard with black shutters, wide floorboards and three fireplaces. It had an amazing history associated with the Unitarian Church and the Underground Railroad. Apparently, the congregants had hidden slaves in the basement before helping them move to Canada and towards freedom. Also, the first doctor in Vermont had lived there, Doctor Powell, he used to make house calls wearing snowshoes. We were a stone's throw away from the Woodstock Green and the Woodstock Inn. Location location location! We used this house year-round. In the summers it was tennis, a little golf, swimming, hiking and working out at the nearby sports center. We climbed Mt. Tom to view the wonderful fall foliage. Gillingham's Shop was where we purchased all our food: meat, maple syrup. But most of all, in winter, we skied as a family at Suicide Six and in Ludlow and Killington, Vermont. We loved skiing as a family. A family that skies together, stays together.

For years, Santa Fe, New Mexico became the destination for our vacations and holidays. In 2004, when Papa retired from Berklee we left Massachusetts, with tears in our eyes, and headed to Santa Fe. We spent three weeks on the road before we reached Santa Fe. On the way, we stopped in places like Louisville, Kentucky and Independence, Missouri where we saw Harry Truman's home and his presidential library. Along the way, we chose to stay in motels based on which one had the best hot breakfast. It was a blast! As a result of home exchanges we did in various parts of the United States, we were able to stay in neighborhoods rather than hotels, feeling what it was like to actually live all around this vast country.

In Santa Fe, we moved to Quail Run a 2,000-square foot home on a golf course, a 2-story townhouse, which we had rented a couple of summers prior. We decorated our Santa Fe home in the Santa Fe style and started collecting pottery and paintings. We had a lot of joy purchasing each piece. Whether pueblo ceramic pots or storyteller dolls, paintings or baskets, we loved everything we brought into our home. In Santa Fe it's inevitable that you become a collector. Everyone would ask us, "What do you collect?" We replied, "We're music people. We support music and musicians, but you can't display that on the wall!"

We now live at Sagewood in Phoenix, Arizona. We de-cluttered and deaccessioned and now we live with only our most favorite possessions in 1240 square feet. We scaled down from 7500 square feet! We've made this place very modern, streamlined and the art is contemporary, regional southwest art. We have some pieces that could be in museum collections.

I'm sitting on the balcony right now listening to the fountain as I record this story for Tania. It is a frog fountain. I'm looking at the Palo Verde trees. We feel secure here. It is quiet. A sanctuary. Here, Papa and I swim daily in the indoor pool; we walk, paint, write, read and organize cultural events.

Home is where the heart is, it's where we hang our hats, where we gather and find peace and quiet and joy. Things happen at home. Reading, piano playing, socializing, inviting friends in for dinner, gathering around a fireplace, eating popcorn, playing music, and celebrating life.

"A chair is still a chair, even when there's no one sittin' there
But a chair is not a house and a house is not a home
When there's no one there to hold you tight
And no one there you can kiss goodnight" —Luther Vandross, A House is not a Home

"The S Word"

The S Word is the title of a documentary made by Emmy award-winning filmmakers Lisa Klein and Doug Blush. The S in the film's title stands for suicide; not a fun topic to talk about, but one that needs to be talked about. I'm 1 of 3 Executive Producers on this film and proud to say that I have been with the project from the very beginning. My relationship with Lisa and Doug started when I heard about their film, *Of Two Minds,* which is about bipolar disorder. Because of my personal connection with bipolar disorder, as well as the many people I have met along the way who also live with this disorder, I decided to bring Doug and the film to Santa Fe and host a screening at the Center for Contemporary Art.

The night of the screening, we served pre-show soup, hors d'oeuvres and nonalcoholic beverages in the Waxman Gallery. Although we had hoped for a full-house, we didn't anticipate having an overflow issue. We had so many people showing up, and due to lack of space, we had to turn some people away.

After the film, there was a panel discussion with two psychiatrists, Dr. Don Fineberg and Dr. Jefferson Davis as well as with Doug, the filmmaker. There were plenty of meaty questions and answers. The event was so well received, that I decided to sign on as an Executive Producer for their next film, *The S Word.*

I've helped raise quite a bit of money for *The S Word* and have introduced the filmmakers to key people who have made their way into the film as supporters and interviewees; as well as finding and creating opportunities and places for the screening of the film. I'm very proud of my association with this film. The film reminds me of my life's work, of the legacy I wish to leave behind, which is that of destigmatizing and demystifying mental illness.

Throughout our lifetime, mental illness will touch all of us in some way. Either directly or indirectly, yet, in our society, so many people choose to sweep it under the rug of politeness or shame. The reality is, that more than 5.7 million American adults are affected by bipolar disorder in any given year (according to National Institute of Mental Health). And millions of people attempt suicide each year with thousands and thousands succeeding. Depression affects more than 350 million people around the world according to the World Health Organization.

Musical Notes: 4

It's no wonder Susan and I share stories about music, my favorite singers are those who tell stories. Patti Griffin, Simon and Garfunkel, Sufjan Stevens, Harry Chapin. When I can see the main character in my mind's eye and feel their hardships, triumphs, joy, as they move through the world of the song… that's my kind of music.

<u>Little Known Music Trivia</u>

"Hey, Mr. Tambourine Man, play a song for me. I'm not sleepy and there ain't no place I'm going to." – Bob Dylan

Do you remember Bob Dylan's song Mr. Tambourine Man? Well, there was a real tambourine man that played a song for Bob Dylan and became the inspiration for the song, "Mr. Tambourine Man" We received a call one day from a music engineer telling us that he was selling the real life tambourine man's tambourine. The tambourine man had fallen into poor health and needed money for medical bills. The tambourine was eventually purchased by the Bob Dylan Archives. Bob Dylan is an icon and won the Nobel Prize in Literature. His songs changed and transcended time.

<u>Birthdays</u>

"They say it's your birthday
It's my birthday too, yeah
They say it's your birthday
We're gonna have a good time
I'm glad it's your birthday
Happy birthday to you" —The Beatles, Birthday song

On February 17, 1942 there was definitely music in the air.

- Huey Newton, the co-founder of the Black Panther Party is born.
- Jazz saxophonist and big band leader, Jimmy Dorsey has a #4 song on the charts, Tangerine.

- Western films like "Cowboy Serenade" and "Arizona Stagecoach" hit the big screen.
- Lee Berk is born, a Jewish cowboy with a love of jazz branded on his heart.

Lee had always envisioned himself studying creative writing at Stanford University and wanted to head out West as soon as he could, but his parents didn't want him to be so far away from them. So, being an only child (and a very responsible one at that) he finally left the East to live in the West after his parents passed away.

In 1992, for Lee's 50th Nancy, Lucy and I gave Lee a Southwest party. We invited 50 guests and hired a scholar from Harvard's Peabody Museum to give a lecture on Native American pottery. After the lecture we presented Lee with an original Hopi pot I had purchased for him at the museum gift shop. He still has that pot.

The day before the party, Lucy, Nancy and I went to visit Terence Janericco a famous chef, cookbook author and cooking instructor who gave us a cooking lesson and then all four of us prepared the hors d'oeuvres and desserts for Lee's party. Terrance brought the food to our home on Hawes Street in Brookline and cooked it on site. I had decorated the tables with Southwest décor; cactus plants and cowboy boot candles. I hired a gospel choral group from Berklee who stood on our magnificent staircase and performed for Lee and our guests.

We have a video of that birthday party. All four of our parents were there, on video, Reggie Laughlin from Berklee interviewed our friends and family. In the video you can see our parents and friends and Lee smiling. I still own the two-piece dark green velvet dress I wore with a silver belt and squash blossom necklace.

Another birthday I remember was when I was a little girl, about 7 or 8 years old, and I was invited to two birthday parties over one weekend. A boy's birthday named Philip Zuckerman and a girl named Sheila Sulman's birthday. For Philip I selected a toolkit and for Sheila a gift of a Betty Crocker baking set. They were both wrapped gifts. When I arrived at the first party, (Phillip's) I present him with one of the wrapped gifts, he opened it, and low and behold… Betty Crocker! Now, in today's day and age where boys cook and girls build houses, that would have been acceptable, but back then, let's just say my face was redder than Betty Crocker's reddest frosting!

I'll never forget Lucy's birthday when we hired a monkey grinder with his monkey for the backyard party in the house on Hawes Street. The monkey tipped his hat, clapped and smiled as we placed coins in his cup encouraging him to play songs.

For one of Nancy's birthdays, we took a boat ride on the Charles River in Boston. We rented a little boat and served a picnic lunch with a beautiful homemade birthday cake. All our cakes were made at the Women's Educational Industrial Union on Boylston Street, which had the finest bakery in the city. Much to my chagrin the WEIU closed down. Known for its golden swan and social values. I took lessons in knitting and needlepoint there and used to buy wonderful gifts from their shop. WEIU honored Amelia Earhart every year. Sad to see good institutions just disappear. In my lifetime you see a lot of change.

Lee's 65th birthday was at the Scottish Rite Temple in Santa Fe, where we brought Kiril Gerstein a Gilmore Prize winner to perform. A classical and jazz graduate from Berklee. Kiril played Gershwin's Rhapsody in Blue (Lee's favorite song) with members of the Santa Fe Symphony. A private party followed the concert with champagne, dessert buffet, and dancing. That's on video too.

As far as your birthdays, we missed out on so many. The Langans, because you were living in Switzerland for 10 years, however, we hope to celebrate more with you now that you live in Portland, Oregon.

For my 60th birthday we celebrated in Santa Fe. I helped to produce a concert, arranging Diana Krall to play at the Santa Fe Opera for the Georgia O'Keeffe Museum's 10th anniversary. My birthday party was held at Vanessie's. We made a video; it was the party of the year.

Noni's Jazz Improvisation

Picture yourself in a sandbox with a sand sifter sifting sand. Say that ten times fast! Well, I sift life experiences; people, places, memories (like birthdays), and music and what remains in my sifter are the golden nuggets. When you think about all the experiences, people, places and music you've experienced and you shake 'em all around your body, which one's stick? What are your gold nuggets? Tell me, I want to know! You know my phone number; just call me up, I'll answer.

Judaism

"Jewish women have always been tellers of stories, across the family table, by a child's bedside, in the kitchen and in countless other intimate situations. Generations of women have used stories to transmit family history, impart values and foster community."

—Jane Guberman, Director of Oral History at Jewish Women's Archives, *In Our Own Voices: A Guide to Conducting Life History Interview with American Jewish Women*

My memoir started as an oral history, with me telling Tania stories face to face or in recordings. The recordings are preserved, so that you can hear my voice, the sound of my subtle Bostonian accent muddled with New London and Santa Fe. In this world of instant messages, emails and cell phones, it's even more important to listen to each other's stories. In sharing my personal and private experiences, my hopes and aspirations, my disappointments and hardships, maybe we can all learn a little something.

In the book *In Our Own Voices* there is a section that explains how to conduct a "community oral history." It says, *One person is the narrator."* (that's me). *The other person is interested in exploring and contributing an interesting perspective.* That's you, Tania. *1. You should encourage your narrator to focus on her own experience rather than those of other people in her life. 2. Explore family and cultural expectations that helped shape your narrator's life choices. 3. Explore particular challenges, obstacles or advantages she faced as a woman. 4. Allow your narrator to follow the flow of her thoughts and freely associate from one story to the next.* I think I'm a master on that one, I associate very freely, I do jump from one thing to another, they often tie together. And Tania has allowed me to jump and feel comfortable with the flow of my thoughts, exploring stories wherever they go or end up. So, thank you Tania for allowing me to be a jumping jack.

Judaism has been a big part of my life and I feel like it's important to share my Jewish stories with you. I'm very proud of my heritage; my grandparents were strong Zionists and believed in Israel. I supported Hadassah (we are five generations of Life Members). From my earliest memories, my family (my mother and grandmothers) lit Friday night candles. We often went to synagogue on Friday nights as well. On Saturdays, we went to synagogue if there was a Bar or Bat Mitzvah. When I was 13 I had a Bat Mitzvah, I wore a burgundy velvet dress. Looking back on my Bat Mitzvah, that ceremony was a significant transition from being a girl to becoming a woman. The ritual solidified my feelings about being Jewish. My Bat Mitzvah was a solo Bat

Mitzvah. I chanted the Haftarah, lit the candles and received silver candlesticks for a job well-done. I still have those candlesticks; they remind me of the moment I became a woman in the Jewish tradition. I think my Bat Mitzvah was Oct. 4th, the same day as my wedding anniversary. I received a Bible, which I still have to this day. I'm a keeper and saver of memories and objects filled with memories. After reading my Torah portion, I gave a brief speech and then joined with three other Bar and Bat Mitzvahs to dance the night away at our collective party at the Shennecossett Golf Club in Groton, Connecticut.

My religious and cultural heritage of Judaism was a combination of my father's orthodox family, and my mother's reformed family. I remember us always having the Jewish National Fund's blue and white charity box in the house. Everyone made at least one trip to Israel. Gussy and Lewis brought back a reproduction of Marc Chagall windows. Even my in-laws (and Lee and I later) helped support The Rimon School of Music in Israel, which trains young people in music. My mother brought back a black wool sleeveless dress decorated with Yemenite silver and gold metal embroidery which I loved and wore often.

We have many scholarships at Berklee for Jewish Israeli students, like Anat Cohen and her two brothers. We've had the Israeli students perform in our home in Brookline and Boston and often invited the Jewish students for Shabbos, Rosh Hashanah, Passover, and Hanukah. We have great memories of this and so do the musical Jewish students. In addition to my Bat Mitzvah I was confirmed, which meant I attended Hebrew school and Sunday School from first grade through high school. I wasn't always a good student, sometimes I behaved badly and caused disturbances. The problem was that we went to Hebrew school after our public-school education and I was tired and simultaneously rambunctious. This combination led to talking a lot, learning a lot and getting in a little bit of trouble. I identify as both a cultural Jew and a religious Jew. United Synagogue Youth (USY) was really important to me growing up. I would spend weekends in West Hartford, Connecticut at my grandparents' (the Millers) home where I would attend USY events with other young Jewish people and even attended a wonderful USY summer camp.

The songs I associated with being Jewish are songs like Hava Nagila, Shabbat shalom, and Lecha Dodi, as well as chanting the blessings over the candles and over the wine and over the bread. I always enjoyed the Hanukkah songs, and loudly sang Dayenu at Passover. Judaism is very musical. Many Jewish cantors became opera singers and there are thousands of Jewish vocalists, performers, vaudevillians, Broadway performers, lyricists, and writers including Allen and Marilyn Bergman and George Gershwin. Judaism helped spawn my love of music. I traveled to Israel in 1968 with my college companion, Betsy. We skipped two weeks in Turkey and Greece so we could spend them in Israel. This was in the summer of 1968 right after the Six-Day War.

Lee and I were married in an orthodox synagogue by a reformed cantor and rabbi, so we blended. The synagogue affiliations we have had were in Temple Israel in Boston and Young Israel in Brookline. I grew up conservative at Beth El synagogue. The big question on Shabbat was: Should I walk to Synagogue or not walk. Now, in Phoenix, we are a part of Congregation Or Tzion.

The negative part of going to synagogue as kids, was that everyone looked at what everyone else was wearing and even if we didn't make comments aloud, we were thinking them! We always wore new hats, new shoes, new dresses. After working though all the "mishigas" of evaluating fellow congregants' attire, I was able to access the joy of attending Temple through the songs, the food, the herring, the chopped liver, the challah bread, the sweet wine, the apples and honey for the new year and dipping the greens in the salt water for the tears of the Jewish people. The symbolism was stunning.

I used to love the Havdalah with the the braided candles. Havdalah is the service at the end of the Sabbath, the blessings that usher us into a new week of the Sabbath on Saturday evenings. My sense of hospitality and love for others comes from Judaism. When Abraham was in his tent, in the desert he washed the feet of visitors, no matter if they were Jewish or not, he invited them in and cared for them. The love of humanity and philanthropy, of giving and charity, of taking care of other people, these are Jewish values and they are a part of me. I'm very grateful to have been born Jewish and happy that my parents and grandparents instilled in me this identity. And I'm happy that my daughters were raised Jewish and might value family and the music. The music is a way to the heart of being Jewish.

Let's not forget about the Jewish holidays! Rosh Hashanah, Yom Kippur, Passover. As a kid, I loved gathering around the table at home, with the special foods like the haroset and gefilte fish. These foods were all made by hand, by my grandmothers' Goldie and Gussie. Goldie also made a sponge cake with a dozen egg yolks that sprung up when you cut into it. It seemed like it was a mile high. And Gussie would make her own gefilte fish with Pike and white fish and both grandmothers would make matzo balls that were light and fluffy. We had the best chicken soup and they would make tender brisket. Even homemade chopped liver left the kitchen and headed right into my tummy. Every single bite was memorable and tasty. I will never forget being young and drinking the sweet Manischewitz wine and falling asleep under the table because the service was so long when Poppop Louie, Dad's father, an orthodox Jew, would lead the service from a to z. The questions, the songs, the discussion, the foods, all of it. At Hanukkah I loved playing dreidel and singing the dreidel song and lighting the candles. We would get one present every day for eight days.

This year at Passover Lee did something so beautiful. He ordered Passover dinner from Zabar's delicatessen in New York and had it flown to both Lucy and Nancy's homes, so we were all eating the same wonderful foods at the same time in our respective homes. A wise deed, indeed!

And now a message to you, our grandchildren, about Judaism, in the form of an email from Lee to Nancy.

From: Lee Berk <leeberk217@gmail.com>
Date: June 23, 2017 at 6:21:15 AM MDT
To: Nancy <n.langan@yahoo.com>
Subject: Fr Dad

When I was a youngster I did not go to Hebrew School, just Sunday School, and I didn't like it. The van would come to our home to pick me up and I would stay in bed until it went away. But my parents did value their Jewish identity and had me tutored to be bar mitzvahed. And you know one of the first questions grand ma Elaine asked when we met was whether I had been bar mitzvahed?

In my parents' era there was still much anti-Semitism. Grandma Alma worked for a judge in Boston and in the insurance industry in New York. She never revealed her religion and it was when my parents returned to Boston they changed their last names to Berk from Berkowitz.

I can still remember going with my mother to my prospective Newton elementary school and my mother asking hesitantly if there were any other Jewish children in the school. This was years before the area became well populated Jewishly and Jews still weren't admitted to the country clubs. My parents eagerly joined the newly formed reform synagogue which at that time was in a private home it had purchased and where I was Bar Mitzvahed. I can still vividly recall reading my Torah portion in Hebrew, speaking my composition, and giving a party in our home for all of my friends.

Even though my parents were not regular attendees, synagogue was important to them. They contributed financially and by producing music shows for the erection of the new synagogue building and we always attended major Jewish holidays there.

There was never any lengthy period in my life that I was not Jewishly affiliated, the last few years being an exception, although even now I have made a generous gift to the conservative synagogue we attend from time to time which has just moved from a rented to a purchased facility and we are considering being members.

Although my Jewishness has waxed and waned over the years, having a strong sense of Jewish identity has always been a central fact of my life. In traveling mom and I almost always visit Jewish sites and in the broader society I always feel a special bond of Jewishness with others of our faith.

I am sure that many of my values of social justice and charity and ethical treatment of others come from what I have studied and learned over time from Jewish history, Torah, rabbinic sermons, the meanings behind the Jewish holidays, and other sources.

So, Nancy, I appreciate your quandary in trying to identify Jewish goals for your children and how best to achieve them. Knowing who I am religiously and its meaning has been and continues to provide a major grounding and enhance in the quality of my life and that of our family including you and Lucy for generations. I certainly hope those benefits can be perpetuated in the lives of your children.

Love,
Dad

Lee is More Than Fine

Love. Love wants to be lofty and to be restrained by nothing lowly. Nothing is sweeter than love, nothing stronger, nothing loftier, nothing grander, fuller, nothing better in heaven or on earth… – Thomas a Kempis, The Imitation of Christ

"He who loves, flies, runs, and rejoices; he is free and nothing holds him back."
–Henri Matisse, *Jazz*

Henri Matisse's book *Jazz* expresses so beautifully how I feel about Lee. Of course this book is the marriage of jazz, poetry and art; that's how I love Lee, at the intersection of jazz, poetry and art. That's how we love each other and there is nothing better in heaven or on earth!

Recently, Tania asked me how Lee is doing, in fact, she asked me twice and I answered, "fine," but really here's how Lee is doing…Lee is delicious!

He's delicious in so many ways. In high school he was captain of the chess team, which sounds nerdy, but it just meant that he was smart, smooth and surprising. Here at Sagewood Lee started a chess club and several men are now playing chess regularly. He's teaching me how to play. He's taught me the difference between the king, pawn and queen. I'm looking forward to learning the game with him. I haven't learned how, yet, because (as you know) it's hard for me to sit still.

He also started Woody's Place here at Sagewood with Martin O'Sullivan, and me. Woody's Place is a virtual jazz club where we book world-class jazz acts eight times a year. We bring national jazz acts to Sagewood and there are almost 150 people in the audience and 180 sponsors. So, Lee is really blossoming between the jazz and chess. He feels delicious when we hold hands.

We met on May 7, 1975; we were married on October 4, 1975. Our wedding song was Minnie Riperton's "Loving You." We've been together over 42 years and are still so much in love, even more so than we have ever been. Lee is handsome, charming, intelligent, very caring and attentive and supportive. We create things together.

When Lee retired in 2004 from being the President of Berklee, we moved to Santa Fe, New Mexico where we created organizations such as the Friends of Santa Fe Jazz. Lee was the Commissioner of Music for the state of New Mexico and founding board member of the New Mexico School of the Arts and I was on the Lensic Performing Art Center's board, the New Mexico Museum Foundation board, and the New Mexico Committee of Women in the Arts, on which I later became president. Eventually we found the town a little too small for all the things we had yet to create, not to mention the uneven healthcare, so we moved to Arizona. We made Mayo Clinic in Arizona our hospital and medical mecca. Here at Sagewood we live just a few miles from the Mayo Clinic hospital campus, so we feel very secure with our medical care. Mayo Clinic has been a great partner in screening films, like *Of Two Minds* and *The S Word* and bringing together panels of psychiatrists and other mental healthcare experts after the screenings to answer questions.

Lee is generous and thoughtful to me, our daughters, and you kids and friends and acquaintances. He's always trying to help people whether it's in a new job or ideas for something and he follows through. He's thriving here in Arizona and if he thrives, I thrive and if I thrive, he thrives. We have a mutual love and respect, which is enduring. We feel very blessed. That's how Lee's doing. We are best friends, lovers, collaborators. At this stage in life, after working and serving on boards and raising a family we are dedicated to spending as much time with each other as possible.
(*This is when your grandmother starts to sing.*)
"*What the world needs now…is love, sweet love…*" and then, "*I always feel I want to say I love you in a song…*"

Music has always been part of our lives and will always be part of our love. Lee is the most honest man I've ever met, kind and thoughtful and respectful. A life of love is like a tree, a very old imposing tall tree, with lots of roots and many branches, and this tree blooms and has fruit. This is our life, a very strong foundation, family is our foundation and the branches are our children, passions, activities, and they bloom and we pass on our strengths, persistence, insights, culture and education. We love looking at trees. We just got back from Connecticut where the trunks and roots of the trees are so strong. The strength of our foundation is in the roots and trunk and new growth, like you kids. And strength is an interesting one because it's easy to feel strong when everything is going well in your life and it's much harder when it's not. Lee and I have been through it all and as George Gershwin sang, *"It's very clear…Our love is here to stay."*

LANES [A Swimmers Dream]
Inspired by The Musical Song
Sung by Joni Mitchell
"Both SIDES Now"

PLANS
PLAINS
PLANES
LANES
          Swimming LANES
          Country LANES
          Bowling LANES
          PRAIRIE PLAINS
PLANES THAT FLY
PLANES THAT Turn (As in woodworking)
And Then There are PLANS

For Me I prefer the Lines,
The Stone walls, The dirt AND
EArth underfoot, The Path.
Robert Frost: "The Path not taken"
"Good Fences mAke good neighbors."

                    Susan Berk

Life's Rhythms

There is a rhythm to life, to living. The way in which we move our bodies, play instruments, sing, sit down for dinner. Rhythms are the patterns that make it possible to understand someone, to melt into a song, to move your body in time to the music. Movement and physical activity have always been so important to me, part of my therapy, just like eating healthy, meditation and mindfulness, too.

Here are some of Noni's musings on the rhythm of health and fitness because both have inspired me to stay afloat in the pool and in life. I love swimming and walking, I've tried skiing and tennis. I loved my bicycle when I was younger it took me to places all over my town; it was freedom, on my own, independence and to ride with others, too. On Saturday afternoons I roller-skated, not only on the sidewalks and streets in front of my home, with metal skates that fit over shoes and used a key to tighten them, but I roller-skated at roller rinks on wooden floors, we went round and round, the boys and girls and the music playing. I used to go bowling with my entire family on Sunday afternoons and with my parents' friends the Bakers and Ritters and their children. And I would cry when I didn't' do well; I was often too self-critical and self-conscious, so a lesson to be learned is don't be self-critical. Enjoy whatever level you can do, participate and find happiness and joy. After bowling we often went for Chinese food or had pizza and grinders. Grinders are what you know of as Subway sandwiches. I loved to eat pizza and popcorn; growing up we popped the popcorn ourselves, almost every Friday or Saturday night at home. One time we had an electric popper. Another time we had one where we roasted the popcorn in the fireplace. I've been a healthy person most of my life because I move my body, by exercising and hiking. At 70 I even weighted the same as I weighted in high school!

Swimming. I love swimming with Lee. We have been swimming together for 42 years. Swimming is how we got to know each other. Being in the pool, in motion, is not stressful; it's rhythmic and meditative. Every job I've had has been close to a pool. Whether at Brandeis or University of Pennsylvania or at the University Club, or Brookline Public High School, Quail Run, Sagewood: Swimming is part of my life. In fact, swimming inspired me to write a poem entitled, "Lanes" which is reproduced at the beginning of this chapter.

Golf. I also play golf; Lee calls me his trophy wife because I once won a golf tournament and was awarded a trophy at Mountain Shadows in Phoenix, Arizona. I was playing in what I like to call, "The Zen Zone" for over three weeks; I played really well. My parents played golf, my brother Marc, brother-in-law, Bill and now my sister Jane play golf. I tried tennis, but I'm not good at chasing things, and tore cartilage in my knee, so I decided not to play. For a long time when I was in Boston I was a runner, waking up early in the morning to run with a group of women and running along the Charles River while practicing for the Bonnie Bell 10k race which I entered and completed.

Biking. I LOVED my bike and when I got older I organized bicycle trips with peers, we went on 20-mile bike rides. I had a bike rack and water bottle and all the right gear. We brought picnic lunches and explored country roads. When I couldn't be outside biking I rode a stationary bike. Exhilarating, joy, releasing tension, all lead to better sleep, a toned body and fuel for thought.

Skiing. I was a little scared of skiing, of going too fast, but loved the scenery, crisp air in New Hampshire, Vermont, New Mexico, it was social too. We skied as a family; Nancy and Lucy learned how to ski well. Lee took up skiing when he was 50 years old. He practiced and had lessons and far surpassed my joy and technique.

Hiking. Lee introduced me to hiking. I was pretty much afraid of the woods, to be out alone, without people and telephones. We started hiking at Mt. Tom in Woodstock, Vermont. In Santa Fe at the ski basin on the Windsor Trail, we explored nature, quiet and peacefulness. Walking is my true love after swimming and growing up in New London meant I could walk everywhere. But Boston was the supreme walking place; I could walk from one end to the other and on my walk, I could see and hear and feel history and art and architecture and people. I got a taste of that when I lived in London, England. Walking has allowed me to see things and smell things that I would have missed if I were in a car or on the subway.

Sailing. I learned to sail as a youngster, we had a red sailfish, it was a lot of fun with a little trepidation. One summer I took sailing lessons at Mitchell College in New London. I was on the sailing team in college and once we sailed against Princeton.

A sports legacy: My mother and father played tennis, rode bikes, played golf, and loved to walk. I've pictured them walking hand in hand many times. Lee's parents were swimmers and walkers too.

Got to Give It Up

"No one has ever become poor by giving." —Anne Frank

I don't have the biggest diamond ring, Lee and I give each other gifts by giving to future generations, to research, to scholarships: that is our diamond ring. I want to talk about scholarships and generosity of the Berk family. We have contributed over 3 million dollars in scholarships to Berklee. For our 40th wedding anniversary we contributed $40,000 to the National Alliance for Mental Illness for a 2-year fund that supported destigmatizing mental illness for young people on college campuses. We supported a filmmaker from Los Angeles who made films about bipolar disorder and suicide. We've been benefactors at Mayo Clinic Hospital. For my 50th birthday Lee made a $50,000 endowment to Massachusetts General Hospital to study bipolar disorder in children. We are regular contributors to McLean, Berklee, Mayo, and other amazing

Institutions, like The Phoenix Symphony, Arizona State University Women and Philanthropy, Musical Instrument Museum, Phoenix Theatre, and the Phoenix Conservatory of Music.

Most couples give each other gifts for special occasions like jewelry or art, but we give each other gifts that will last longer and have much deeper roots. We give gifts of education, arts and music. I'll take a scholarship that helps young people develop musical skills over a fancy watch any day! However, sometimes I've received both!

<u>Beauty</u>

"I'm beautiful, I'm beautiful, I'm beautiful, dammit!" –Bette Midler
"The beauty of jazz is that it's malleable. People are addressing it to suit their own personalities." —Pat Metheny

The saying goes: Beauty is in the eye of the beholder. The beholder can be others and it can be self. With love and support from parents, children can create a feeling of beauty and self, inside them. Without all of the support, love and nurturing, then the notion of beauty becomes clouded. I never felt pretty. But now I do. Why? Why the change? Well, one reason has been therapy. I used to be self-conscious about singing off key or doing the wrong dance steps, however, over time I began to feel like my life is here to be lived. I'm here to celebrate it. I'm older and wiser and I respect myself. Through Lee's love and support and nurturing for all these years, plus friends and psychoanalysis, I've come to feel beautiful. Less critical about myself and others. I want to thank Lee. This section is inspired by Meryl Streep. In her acceptance speech for an Oscar, the first person she thanks is her husband, Don Gummer, who is a sculptor. Meryl and Don have been married 38 years. I want Lee to know that I echo Meryl Streep's words, "Everything I value most in our lives, you've given me." I look at Lee and I feel beautiful, in fact, at this moment, I feel the best I've ever felt. And even though we fell in love and married within a few months, it's all the years of togetherness. We came from different families, with different backgrounds and created our own style together. We've worked and developed as individuals and as a couple. Lee is beautiful in my eyes. And I'm beautiful in his. Our daughters and sons-in-law and grandchildren are all beautiful people. I'm very proud of our family. Whenever I spend time with you, it seems like you've inherited this legacy of love, positive attitude and respect and caring for yourselves and other people.

The Way We Are

"We are all descended from ancestors who loved music and dance, storytelling, and spirituality."
– Daniel J. Levitin, The World in Six Songs

This is a poem I wrote inspired by Barbra Streisand's song *The Way We Were.*

"The Challenge of Aging"

Thinning grey hair
Freckles that are suspicious that turn into Basel cells, atypical cells even melanoma
The browning of my once white teeth
Receding gums
Diminished eyesight
Forgetfulness
Changing sleep habits

My husband's hearing loss
My husband's idiopathic neuropathy
My husband's pacemaker and silent
heart attack

The Way we were
Life was so simple then

Our daughters becoming wives and mothers
And sometimes not agreeing with their parenting
Seeing friends get sick.....die
Losing friends

How we "see" ourselves

How we feel
Resolving the differences

Having "episodes" doing our most favorite things
Living long enough to see our main meds
Become generic
Yet still realize their mysteries-of life
Guessing
No sure answers
Not Black and white
The gray of life

Susan Berk
April 2017

But Not The End

"The memory of things gone is important to a jazz musician. Things like old folks singing in the moonlight in the back yard on a hot night or something said long ago."
—Louis Armstrong

"I think this memoir is going to have a beginning, but not an end."
—Susan Berk

Music is your inheritance. It's time to drop the needle on your life and listen to the stories your parent's long to tell you, listen to each other, close your eyes and listen to the sound the wind makes outside your bedroom window when you can't sleep because it's the night before school starts and you're a little nervous. Listen to your grandparents, listen to your hearts. This is your polyphonic life. This is jazz. It's time to improvise!

A FAMILY ALBUM

SUGAR LEE

88

NANCY WITH THE SHINING EYES

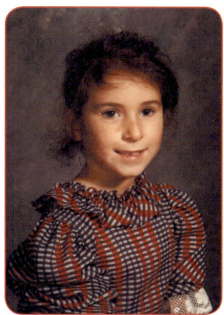

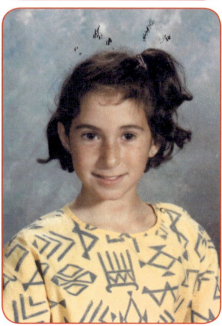

Lucy in the Sky with Diamonds

HOME ON THE RANGE

David & Gussie

Gussie & David

George

Larry

David

94

Alma & Larry

David & Elaine

Jaguar

Larry with Jimmy Carter

Goldie & Elaine

Song for Susan

Susan Berk

Susan & Jane

David & Susan

Susan & Jane

Susan with Larry and Alma

Lee, Susan, Barbara and Marc

LOVE AND MARRIAGE

Lee, Susan, James Taylor and Natalie Cole

Susa, Lee and James Taylor